Neoliberalism: A Very Short Introduction

VERY SHORT INTRODUCTIONS are for anyone wanting a stimulating and accessible way into a new subject. They are written by experts, and have been translated into more than 45 different languages.

The series began in 1995, and now covers a wide variety of topics in every discipline. The VSI library now contains over 500 volumes—a Very Short Introduction to everything from Psychology and Philosophy of Science to American History and Relativity—and continues to grow in every subject area.

Titles in the series include the following:

AFRICAN HISTORY John Parker and Richard Rathbone
AMERICAN HISTORY Paul S. Boyer
AMERICAN LEGAL HISTORY G. Edward White
AMERICAN POLITICAL PARTIES AND ELECTIONS L. Sandy Maisel
AMERICAN POLITICS Richard M. Valelly
AMERICAN SLAVERY Heather Andrea Williams
ANARCHISM Colin Ward
ANCIENT EGYPT Ian Shaw
ANCIENT GREECE Paul Cartledge
ANCIENT PHILOSOPHY Julia Annas
ANCIENT WARFARE Harry Sidebottom
ANGLICANISM Mark Chapman
THE ANGLO-SAXON AGE John Blair
ANIMAL RIGHTS David DeGrazia
ARCHAEOLOGY Paul Bahn
ARISTOTLE Jonathan Barnes
ART HISTORY Dana Arnold
ART THEORY Cynthia Freeland
ATHEISM Julian Baggini
THE ATMOSPHERE Paul I. Palmer
AUGUSTINE Henry Chadwick
BACTERIA Sebastian G. B. Amyes
BEAUTY Roger Scruton
THE BIBLE John Riches
BLACK HOLES Katherine Blundell
BLOOD Chris Cooper
THE BRAIN Michael O'Shea
THE BRICS Andrew F. Cooper
BRITISH POLITICS Anthony Wright

BUDDHA Michael Carrithers
BUDDHISM Damien Keown
BUDDHIST ETHICS Damien Keown
CAPITALISM James Fulcher
CATHOLICISM Gerald O'Collins
THE CELTS Barry Cunliffe
CHOICE THEORY Michael Allingham
CHRISTIANITY Linda Woodhead
CIRCADIAN RHYTHMS Russell Foster and Leon Kreitzman
CITIZENSHIP Richard Bellamy
CLASSICAL MYTHOLOGY Helen Morales
CLASSICS Mary Beard and John Henderson
CLIMATE CHANGE Mark Maslin
THE COLD WAR Robert McMahon
COMMUNISM Leslie Holmes
CONSCIOUSNESS Susan Blackmore
CONTEMPORARY ART Julian Stallabrass
COSMOLOGY Peter Coles
THE CRUSADES Christopher Tyerman
DADA AND SURREALISM David Hopkins
DARWIN Jonathan Howard
THE DEAD SEA SCROLLS Timothy Lim
DECOLONIZATION Dane Kennedy
DEMOCRACY Bernard Crick
DESIGN John Heskett
DREAMING J. Allan Hobson
DRUGS Les Iversen
THE EARTH Martin Redfern

ECONOMICS Partha Dasgupta
EGYPTIAN MYTH Geraldine Pinch
THE ELEMENTS Philip Ball
EMOTION Dylan Evans
EMPIRE Stephen Howe
ENGLISH LITERATURE Jonathan Bate
ETHICS Simon Blackburn
EUGENICS Philippa Levine
THE EUROPEAN UNION John Pinder
and Simon Usherwood
EVOLUTION Brian and Deborah
Charlesworth
EXISTENTIALISM Thomas Flynn
FASCISM Kevin Passmore
FEMINISM Margaret Walters
THE FIRST WORLD WAR
Michael Howard
FORENSIC PSYCHOLOGY
David Canter
FOUCAULT Gary Gutting
FREE SPEECH Nigel Warburton
FREE WILL Thomas Pink
FREUD Anthony Storr
FUNDAMENTALISM Malise Ruthven
FUNGI Nicholas P. Money
GALAXIES John Gribbin
GALILEO Stillman Drake
GAME THEORY Ken Binmore
GANDHI Bhikhu Parekh
GEOGRAPHY John Matthews and
David Herbert
GEOPOLITICS Klaus Dodds
GLOBAL CATASTROPHES
Bill McGuire
GLOBAL ECONOMIC HISTORY
Robert C. Allen
GLOBALIZATION Manfred Steger
HABERMAS James Gordon Finlayson
HEGEL Peter Singer
HINDUISM Kim Knott
THE HISTORY OF LIFE Michael Benton
THE HISTORY OF MATHEMATICS
Jacqueline Stedall
THE HISTORY OF
MEDICINE William Bynum
THE HISTORY OF TIME
Leofranc Holford-Strevens
HIV AND AIDS Alan Whiteside
HOLLYWOOD Peter Decherney
HUMAN EVOLUTION Bernard Wood

HUMAN RIGHTS Andrew Clapham
IDEOLOGY Michael Freeden
INDIAN PHILOSOPHY Sue Hamilton
INFINITY Ian Stewart
INFORMATION Luciano Floridi
INNOVATION Mark Dodgson and
David Gann
INTELLIGENCE Ian J. Deary
INTERNATIONAL MIGRATION
Khalid Koser
INTERNATIONAL RELATIONS
Paul Wilkinson
ISLAM Malise Ruthven
ISLAMIC HISTORY Adam Silverstein
JESUS Richard Bauckham
JOURNALISM Ian Hargreaves
JUDAISM Norman Solomon
JUNG Anthony Stevens
KANT Roger Scruton
KNOWLEDGE Jennifer Nagel
THE KORAN Michael Cook
LAW Raymond Wacks
THE LAWS OF THERMODYNAMICS
Peter Atkins
LEADERSHIP Keith Grint
LINGUISTICS Peter Matthews
LITERARY THEORY Jonathan Culler
LOCKE John Dunn
LOGIC Graham Priest
MACHIAVELLI Quentin Skinner
MARX Peter Singer
MATHEMATICS Timothy Gowers
THE MEANING OF LIFE
Terry Eagleton
MEASUREMENT David Hand
MEDICAL ETHICS Tony Hope
MEDIEVAL BRITAIN John Gillingham
and Ralph A. Griffiths
MEMORY Jonathan K. Foster
METAPHYSICS Stephen Mumford
MILITARY JUSTICE Eugene R. Fidell
MODERN ART David Cottington
MODERN CHINA Rana Mitter
MODERN IRELAND Senia Pašeta
MODERN ITALY Anna Cento Bull
MODERN JAPAN
Christopher Goto-Jones
MODERNISM Christopher Butler
MOLECULES Philip Ball
MOONS David A. Rothery

MUSIC Nicholas Cook
MYTH Robert A. Segal
NEOLIBERALISM Manfred Steger and
    Ravi Roy
NIETZSCHE Michael Tanner
NORTHERN IRELAND
    Marc Mulholland
NOTHING Frank Close
THE PALESTINIAN-ISRAELI
    CONFLICT Martin Bunton
PANDEMICS Christian W. McMillen
PARTICLE PHYSICS Frank Close
PHILOSOPHY Edward Craig
PHILOSOPHY OF LAW
    Raymond Wacks
PHILOSOPHY OF SCIENCE
    Samir Okasha
PHOTOGRAPHY Steve Edwards
PLATO Julia Annas
POLITICAL PHILOSOPHY David Miller
POLITICS Kenneth Minogue
POSTCOLONIALISM Robert Young
POSTMODERNISM Christopher Butler
POSTSTRUCTURALISM
    Catherine Belsey
PREHISTORY Chris Gosden
PRESOCRATIC PHILOSOPHY
    Catherine Osborne
PSYCHIATRY Tom Burns
PSYCHOLOGY Gillian Butler and
    Freda McManus
QUANTUM THEORY
    John Polkinghorne
RACISM Ali Rattansi
THE REFORMATION Peter Marshall
RELATIVITY Russell Stannard
THE RENAISSANCE Jerry Brotton
RENAISSANCE ART
    Geraldine A. Johnson
REVOLUTIONS Jack A. Goldstone
RHETORIC Richard Toye
RISK Baruch Fischhoff and John Kadvany
RITUAL Barry Stephenson

RIVERS Nick Middleton
ROBOTICS Alan Winfield
ROMAN BRITAIN Peter Salway
THE ROMAN EMPIRE
    Christopher Kelly
THE ROMAN REPUBLIC
    David M. Gwynn
RUSSIAN HISTORY Geoffrey Hosking
THE RUSSIAN REVOLUTION
    S. A. Smith
SCHIZOPHRENIA Chris Frith and
    Eve Johnstone
SCIENCE AND RELIGION
    Thomas Dixon
SEXUALITY Véronique Mottier
SIKHISM Eleanor Nesbitt
SLEEP Steven W. Lockley and
    Russell G. Foster
SOCIAL AND CULTURAL
    ANTHROPOLOGY
    John Monaghan and Peter Just
SOCIALISM Michael Newman
SOCIOLOGY Steve Bruce
SOCRATES C. C. W. Taylor
SOUND Mike Goldsmith
THE SOVIET UNION Stephen Lovell
STATISTICS David J. Hand
STUART BRITAIN John Morrill
TELESCOPES Geoff Cottrell
THEOLOGY David F. Ford
TIBETAN BUDDHISM
    Matthew T. Kapstein
THE TUDORS John Guy
THE UNITED NATIONS
    Jussi M. Hanhimäki
THE VIKINGS Julian Richards
VIRUSES Dorothy H. Crawford
WAR AND TECHNOLOGY
    Alex Roland
WILLIAM SHAKESPEARE
    Stanley Wells
THE WORLD TRADE
    ORGANIZATION Amrita Narlikar

Manfred B. Steger and Ravi K. Roy

NEOLIBERALISM

A Very Short Introduction

OXFORD
UNIVERSITY PRESS

OXFORD
UNIVERSITY PRESS

Great Clarendon Street, Oxford OX2 6DP

Oxford University Press is a department of the University of Oxford.
It furthers the University's objective of excellence in research, scholarship,
and education by publishing worldwide in

Oxford New York

Auckland Cape Town Dar es Salaam Hong Kong Karachi
Kuala Lumpur Madrid Melbourne Mexico City Nairobi
New Delhi Shanghai Taipei Toronto

With offices in

Argentina Austria Brazil Chile Czech Republic France Greece
Guatemala Hungary Italy Japan Poland Portugal Singapore
South Korea Switzerland Thailand Turkey Ukraine Vietnam

Oxford is a registered trade mark of Oxford University Press
in the UK and in certain other countries

Published in the United States
by Oxford University Press Inc., New York

British Library Cataloguing in Publication Data

Data available

Library of Congress Cataloging in Publication Data

Data available

Typeset by SPI Publisher Services, Pondicherry, India
Printed in Great Britain
on acid-free paper by
Ashford Colour Press Ltd, Gosport, Hampshire

ISBN 978-0-19-956051-6

Contents

Preface ix

Abbreviations xiii

List of illustrations xv

List of figures xvii

List of maps xviii

1 What's 'neo' about liberalism? 1

2 First-wave neoliberalism in the 1980s: Reaganomics and Thatcherism 21

3 Second-wave neoliberalism in the 1990s: Clinton's market globalism and Blair's Third Way 50

4 Neoliberalism and Asian development 76

5 Neoliberalism in Latin America and Africa 98

6 Crises of neoliberalism: the 2000s and beyond 119

References 138

Index 145

Preface

The 21st-century world is a fundamentally interdependent place.
Globalization has expanded, intensified, and accelerated social
relations across world-time and world-space. The digital
revolution has served as a catalyst for the creation of sprawling
information and communication networks that enmesh
individuals, states, and businesses alike. Transnational terrorist
cells capable of acting anywhere have targeted symbols of secular
power and prompted Western political leaders to declare a 'global
war on terror'. Global climate change and global pandemics have
become a frightening reality, forcing countries to work out a
common strategy aimed at preventing a catastrophe of planetary
proportions. The bursting of the US housing bubble has triggered a
global financial crisis that has wiped out trillions of dollars of assets
worldwide and pushed the international community to the brink of
yet another Great Depression. Triumphalist voices who once saw
the collapse of Soviet communism as the 'end of history' and the
beginning of the unchallenged rule of American-style free-market
capitalism have been silenced as the new century has remained an
ideological battlefield where all kinds of competing political
ideologies vie for the hearts and minds of a global audience.

'Neoliberalism' is one of these new 'isms'. The term was first coined
in post-World War I Germany by a small circle of economists and
legal scholars affiliated with the 'Freiburg School' to refer to their

moderate programme of reviving classical liberalism. In the 1970s, a group of Latin American economists adopted *neoliberalismo* for their pro-market model. By early 1990s, however, left-leaning critics of market reform in the global South had imbued 'neoliberalism' with pejorative meanings associated with the 'Washington Consensus' – a set of economic institutions and policies alleged to have been designed by the United States to globalize American capitalism and its associated cultural system. Other critics dismissed 'neoliberalism' as an opaque catchphrase invented by radical academics or reactionary economic nationalists for the purpose of downgrading the intellectual achievements of neoclassical economists such as Nobel-prize winners Milton Friedman and Friedrich von Hayek. Still others saw it as a postmodern version of quaint 18th-century *'laissez-faire* talk' glorifying individual self-interest, economic efficiency, and unbridled competition. In spite of these criticisms, however, neoliberalism has stuck in the public mind. Today, it appears almost daily in the headlines of the world's major newspapers.

Over the last quarter century, 'neoliberalism' has been associated with such different political figures as Ronald Reagan, Margaret Thatcher, Bill Clinton, Tony Blair, Augusto Pinochet, Boris Yeltsin, Jiang Zemin, Manmohan Singh, Junichiro Koizumi, John Howard, and George W. Bush. But not one of these political leaders has ever publicly embraced this ambiguous label – although they all share some affinity for 'neoliberal' policies aimed at deregulating national economies, liberalizing international trade, and creating a single global market. In its heyday during the 1990s, neoliberalism bestrode the world like a colossus. It ate its way into the heart of the former Soviet bloc. It confronted countries of the global South with the new rules and conditions for their economic development. Showing itself to be a remarkably versatile creature, neoliberalism even charmed the post-Mao Chinese Communist Party cadres whose reformed 'socialism with Chinese characteristics' looks suspiciously like its supposed ideological nemesis.

At the dawn of the new century, however, neoliberalism has been discredited as the global economy built on its principles has been shaken to its core by a financial calamity not seen since the dark years of the 1930s. Is neoliberalism doomed or will it regain its former glory? Will reform-minded G-20 leaders embark on a genuinely new course or try to claw their way back to the neoliberal glory days of the Roaring Nineties? Is there a viable alternative to neoliberalism?

Culminating in a brief reflection on these crucial questions, this book has been designed to introduce readers to the origins, evolution, and core ideas of neoliberalism by examining its concrete manifestations in various countries and regions around the world. Our exploration will show that although neoliberals across the globe share a common belief in the power of 'self-regulating' free markets to create a better world, their doctrine comes in different hues and multiple variations. Reaganomics, for example, is not exactly the same as Thatcherism. Bill Clinton's brand of market globalism diverges in some respects from Tony Blair's Third Way. And political elites in the global South (often educated at the elite universities of the North) have learned to fit the dictates of the Washington Consensus to match their own local contexts and political objectives. Thus, neoliberalism has adapted to specific environments, problems, and opportunities. For this reason, it makes sense to think of our subject in the plural – *neoliberalisms* rather than a single monolithic manifestation.

The main ideas, policies, and modes of governance fuelling these neoliberal projects lie at the heart of this volume. Carrying out our publisher's wish to keep this introduction *very short*, we are forced to engage in a rather selective and general discussion. Its main purpose is to present an accessible and informative – but bare – outline of a rich and complex phenomenon. Readers who have digested the materials offered here and feel prepared to delve more deeply into our subject are advised to consult the concluding reference section.

We would like to thank the Global Cities Research Institute and the Globalism Research Centre at the Royal Melbourne Institute of Technology (RMIT University), as well as the Australian Research Council (ARC) for providing us with valuable research support. We also appreciate the helping hands extended to us by our colleagues and friends affiliated with RMIT University, the University of Hawai'i-Manoa, Claremont Graduate University, the University of California at Santa Barbara, the Shanghai Academy of the Social Sciences, the Free University Berlin, and the University of Oxford. Andrea Keegan and her able team at Oxford University Press have been wonderful to work with. But most of all, we wish to thank our respective families for their enduring love and support. Perle, Joan, and Nicole, this book is for you! Many people have contributed to making this a better book; its remaining shortcomings are our sole responsibility.

Abbreviations

ARC	Australian Research Council
AT&T	American Telephone and Telegraph
CCP	Chinese Communist Party
CIA	Central Intelligence Agency
DLC	Democratic Leadership Council
EPA	Environmental Protection Agency
ERM	Exchange Rate Mechanism
EU	European Union
FDR	Franklin D. Roosevelt
FTA	Free Trade Agreement
FTAA	Free Trade Area of the Americas
G-7	Group of Seven
G-20	Group of Twenty
GATT	General Agreement on Tariffs and Trade
GDP	Gross Domestic Product
GRH	Gramm-Rudman-Hollings Initiative
HDI	Human Development Index
HIPCs	Heavily Indebted Poor Countries
IMF	International Monetary Fund
LDP	Liberal Democratic Party (Japan)
MITI	Ministry of International Trade and Industry (Japan)
MOF	Ministry of Finance (Japan)
MTFS	Medium Term Financial Strategy

NAFTA	North American Free Trade Agreement
NATO	North Atlantic Treaty Organization
NHS	(British) National Health Service
PPP	Purchasing Price Parity Index
PRI	Institutional Revolutionary Party (Mexico)
SAPs	Structural Adjustment Programmes
S&L	Savings and Loans Industry
SEZs	Special Enterprise Zones
SOEs	State-Owned Enterprises
TNC	Transnational Corporation
TRIPs	Trade-Related Aspects of Intellectual Property Rights
US	United States (of America)
USSR	Union of Soviet Socialist Republics
WTO	World Trade Organization

Neoliberalism

List of illustrations

1 President Barack Obama delivering his 2009 Inaugural Address, 20 January 2009 **2**
© Rich Friedman/Corbis

2 Adam Smith (1723–90) **4**
Courtesy of the Adam Smith Institute

3 John Maynard Keynes (1883–1946) **8**
© Hulton Archives/Getty Images

4 Friedrich August von Hayek (1899–1992) **16**
© Hulton Archive/Getty Images

5 Milton Friedman (1912–2006) **18**
© Bettmann/Corbis

6 Ronald Wilson Reagan (1911–2004), 40th President of the United States of America (1981–9) **26**
Courtesy of the Library of Congress

7 Michael Douglas as financial tycoon Gordon Gekko in *Wall Street*: 'Greed is good' **32**
© Collection Cinéma Photos12.com

8 Margaret Hilda Thatcher (1925–), Prime Minister of the United Kingdom (1979–90) **39**
© Manchester Daily Express/Science & Society Picture Library

9 Reagan and Gorbachev shaking hands at their 1988 summit in Moscow after exchanging ratifications of the Intermediate Nuclear Force Treaty **48**
© RIA Novosli/TopFoto

10 President Bill Clinton and British Prime Minister Tony Blair in conversation at 'Roundtable Discussion on the Third Way: Progressive Governance for the 21st Century', held

on 25 April 1999 in
Washington, DC 52
© Getty Images

11 Junichiro Koizumi (1932–),
    Prime Minister of Japan
    (2001–6) 82
    © AFP/Getty Images

12 Chinese Leader Deng
    Xiaoping (1904–97) 85
    © Hulton Archive/Getty Images

13 Manmohan Singh (1932–),
    Prime Minister of India

(2004–) 95
© AP/Press Association Images

14 Ernesto Zedillo Ponce
    de Léon (1951–),
    President of Mexico
    (1994–2000) 109
    © AP/Press Association Images

15 Jeremiah (Jerry) Rawlings
    (1947–); Ghana's Head
    of State (1979; 1981–93);
    President of Ghana
    (1993–2001) 113
    © 2004 UPP/TopFoto

List of figures

A. Reaganomics and Thatcherism: supply-side and monetarist neoliberalism   25

B. The best-paid US CEOs, 1996   61

C. Average hourly earnings of non-supervisory employees in private, non-farm employment, 1950–97   62

D. Household shares of aggregate income in the US, 1967–2003   63

E. The Big Mac Index and the overvalued Yuan   89

F. India's GDP growth rate, 2006–9   94

G. The 15 most unequal nations in the world   101

H. Ghana's Human Development Index, 2005   116

I. 2008 compensation packages (salary, bonuses, and stock options) of the top-ten US CEOs   128

J. Global financial crisis: losses and bailouts for US and European countries in context   129

K. The collapse of world trade   132

L. The contraction of the world economy   132

List of maps

1. China's Special Enterprise Zones   88
2. Countries falling into recession as a result of the global financial crisis   130

Chapter 1
What's 'neo' about liberalism?

Liberalism old and new

Delivering his 2009 Inaugural Address in the throes of the worst economic crisis since the Great Depression of the 1930s, Barack Obama minced no words as he pointed his finger at what he considered to be the chief culprits of the global financial disaster: greed and irresponsibility on the part of some, and people's collective failure to make hard choices and prepare themselves for a new age. Expanding his argument, the youthful President insisted that the key question today was no longer whether government was too big or too small, but whether it worked. Then, looking straight into cameras that projected his stern image onto countless TV and computer screens around the world, the American leader took issue with the reigning economic paradigm of the last 30 years:

> Nor is the question before us whether the market is a force for good or ill. Its power to generate wealth and expand freedom is unmatched. But this crisis has reminded us that without a watchful eye, the market can spin out of control.

The reaction from news pundits was swift and unambiguous: Obama's address was a clear indication that the age of 'neoliberalism' might be coming to an end.

1. President Barack Obama delivering his 2009 Inaugural Address

To be sure, the object of the President's criticism – the neoliberal ideal of the 'self-regulating market' as the main engine powering the individual's rational pursuit of wealth – had been a core tenet of economists since the late 18th century. Opposed to the mercantilism of monarchs who exercised almost total control over the economy in their efforts to amass large quantities of gold for largely bellicose purposes, 'classical liberals' like Adam Smith and David Ricardo preached the virtues of the 'free market' and '*laissez-faire*' economics. Smith is credited with creating the Scottish Enlightenment image of *homo economicus* – the view that people are isolated individuals whose actions reflect mostly their material

2

self-interests. According to this view, economic and political matters are largely separable, with economics claiming a superior status because it operates best without government interference under a harmonious system of natural laws. Thus, the state is to refrain from 'interfering' with the economic activities of self-interested citizens and instead use its power to guarantee open economic exchange.

Ricardo's theory of 'comparative advantage' became the gospel of modern free traders. He argued that free trade amounted to a win-win situation for all trading partners involved, because it allowed each country to specialize in the production of those commodities for which it had a comparative advantage. For example, if Italy could produce wine more cheaply than England, and England could produce cloth more cheaply than Italy, then both countries would benefit from specialization and trade. In fact, Ricardo even went so far as to suggest that benefits from specialization and trade would accrue even if one country had an absolute advantage in producing all of the products traded. Politically, Ricardo's theory amounted to a powerful argument against government interference with trade and was used by 19th-century liberals like Richard Cobden as a formidable ideological weapon in the struggle to repeal the protectionist Corn Laws in England.

For classical liberals, producers were the servants of consumers who pursued their material needs and wants as they saw fit. Dedicated to the protection of private property and the legal enforcement of contracts, classical liberals argued that the 'invisible hand' of the market ensured the most efficient and effective allocation of resources while facilitating peaceful commercial intercourse among nations. Their ideas proved to be a potent force in fomenting the great 18th-century revolutions that toppled royal dynasties, separated church and state, and shattered the dogmas of mercantilism. For most of the 19th century, the heirs of classical liberalism sought to convince people that bad economic times always reflected some form of 'government failure' – usually too much state interference resulting in distorted price signals.

2. Adam Smith (1723–90)

Classical liberalism and the Enlightenment

Classical liberalism arose in tandem with the Enlightenment movement of the late 17th and the 18th centuries which proclaimed reason as the foundation of individual freedom. Enlightenment thinkers like John Locke (1632–1704) argued that in the 'state of nature', all men were free and equal, therefore possessing inalienable rights independent of the laws of any government or authority. Naturally endowed with the right to life, liberty, and property, humans could legitimately establish only *limited* governments whose chief task consisted of securing and protecting these individual rights, especially private property.

How could there be such a thing as 'market failure', they reasoned, if markets – properly shielded from the meddling state – were by nature incapable of 'failing'?

But the turbulent 20th century soon cast a dark cloud on these 'truths' of classical liberalism. It wasn't until the 1980s that 'neoliberals' managed to bring back some of these quaint ideas – albeit dressed in new garments. So what happened in the intervening period? The story is well known. The fury and longevity of the Great Depression convinced leading economic thinkers like John Maynard Keynes and Karl Polanyi that government was much more than a mere 'night watchman' – the role assigned to the state by classical liberals. At the same time, however, Keynes and his new breed of 'egalitarian liberals' disagreed with Marxists who saw the persistence of economic crises as evidence for the coming collapse of capitalism and the victory of a 'revolutionary proletariat' that had seen through the 'ideological distortions' of the 'ruling bourgeoisie': never again would workers fall into the clever trap of accepting their own exploitation in the name of high-sounding liberal ideals like 'freedom', 'opportunity', and 'hard work'. Seeking to prevent revolution by means of economic reform, egalitarian liberals like Prime Minister Clement Atlee and President Franklin D. Roosevelt remained staunch defenders of individual autonomy and property rights. And yet, they criticized classical liberalism for its inability to recognize that modern capitalism had to be subjected to certain regulations and controls by a strong secular state.

Keynes, in particular, advocated massive government spending in a time of economic crisis to create new jobs and lift consumer spending. Thus, he challenged classical liberal beliefs that the market mechanism would naturally correct itself in the event of an economic crisis and return to an equilibrium at full employment. Keynes linked unemployment to a shortage of private capital investment and spending in the economy. For this shortfall, he blamed short-sighted and avaricious investors, whose speculative investments had destabilized the market. Committed to the market principle but opposed to the 'free market', 'Keynesianism' even called for some state ownership of crucial national enterprises like railroads or energy companies.

Keynes led the British delegation at the 1944 Bretton Woods Conference in the United States, which established the post-war international economic order and its international economic institutions. The International Monetary Fund (IMF) was created to administer the international monetary system. The International Bank for Reconstruction and Development, later known as the World Bank, was initially designed to provide loans for Europe's postwar reconstruction. During the 1950s, however, its purpose was expanded to fund various industrial projects in developing countries around the world. Finally, the General Agreement on Tariffs and Trade (GATT) was established in 1947 as a global trade organization charged with fashioning and enforcing multilateral trade agreements. In 1995, the World Trade Organization (WTO) was founded as the successor organization to GATT and subsequently became the focal point of intense public controversy over its neoliberal design of free trade agreements.

The political applications of Keynesian ideas inspired what some economists called the 'golden age of controlled capitalism', which lasted roughly from 1945 to 1975. The American 'New Deal' and 'Great Society' programmes spearheaded by FDR and President Lyndon Johnson, the much admired model of Swedish social democracy, and the British version of 'welfarism' launched in 1945 reflected a broad political consensus among Western nations that led some pundits to proclaim the 'end of ideology'. National governments controlled money flows in and out of their territories. High taxation on wealthy individuals and profitable corporations led to the expansion of the welfare state. Rising wages and increased social services in the wealthy countries of the global North offered workers entry into the middle class.

The golden age of controlled capitalism in the United States

The economy was based on mass production. Mass production was profitable because a large middle class had enough money to purchase what could be mass produced. The middle class had the money because the profits from mass production were divided up between giant corporations and their suppliers, retailers, and employees. The bargaining power of this latter group was enhanced and enforced by government action. Almost a third of the workforce belonged to a union. Economic benefits were also spread across the nation – to farmers, veterans, smaller towns, and small business – through regulation (of railroads, telephones, utilities, and small business) and subsidy (price supports, highways, federal loans).

Source: Robert B. Reich, *Supercapitalism: The Transformation of Business, Democracy, and Everyday Life* (New York: Knopf, 2008), p. 17

3. John Maynard Keynes (1883–1946)

Even US President Richard Nixon, a conservative Republican, proclaimed as late as 1970 that 'we are all Keynesians now'. It was the Keynesian advocacy of an interventionist state and regulated markets that gave 'liberalism' its modern economic meaning: a doctrine favouring a large, active government, regulation of

Keynesian macroeconomics

John Maynard Keynes's literary masterpiece, *The General Theory of Employment, Interest and Money*, was published in 1936 at the height of the Great Depression. The book gained instant prominence because it successfully challenged classical liberal ideas about how modern economies worked. Keynesian ideas proved to be crucial in the development of the theoretical framework of 'macroeconomics'. This new field proclaimed that it was possible for national governments to aggregate data and predict economic crises in advance of their occurrence, thus proposing the use of various policies to intervene in and make adjustments to the economy. Specifically, governments were to increase public spending during economic recessions in order to spur growth, and reduce spending during periods of boom in order to keep inflation in check. Keynesian ideas dominated macroeconomics until the rise of neoliberal doctrines in the early 1970s.

industry, high taxes for the rich, and extensive social welfare programmes for all.

In the three decades following World War II, modern egalitarian liberalism delivered spectacular economic growth rates, high wages, low inflation, and unprecedented levels of material wellbeing and social security. But this golden age of controlled capitalism ground to a halt with the severe economic crises of the 1970s. In response to such unprecedented calamities as 'oil shocks' that quadrupled the price of petrol overnight, the simultaneous occurrence of runaway inflation and rising unemployment ('stagflation'), and falling corporate profits, an entirely new breed of liberals sought a way forward by reviving the old doctrine of classical liberalism under the novel conditions of globalization.

These 'neoliberals' subscribed to a common set of ideological and political principles dedicated to the worldwide spread of an economic model emphasizing free markets and free trade. And yet, they emphasized different parts of their theory according to their particular social contexts. Worshipped by their followers and detested by the Keynesians, neoliberals succeeded in the early 1980s in setting the world's economic and political agenda for the next quarter century. As we shall discuss in Chapters 2 and 3, they argued that crippling government regulation, exorbitant public spending, and high tariff barriers to international trade had been responsible for creating conditions that led to high inflation and poor economic growth throughout the industrial countries in the 1970s. Once this premise became widely accepted, it was the logical next step to claim that these factors remained the major impediment to successful economic development in the global South. Thus was born a global neoliberal development agenda based primarily on so-called 'structural adjustment programmes' and international free-trade agreements. As we shall see in Chapters 4 and 5, powerful economic institutions like the International Monetary Fund and the World Bank imposed their neoliberal agenda on heavily indebted developing countries in return for much-needed loans. The 1991 demise of the Soviet Union and the acceleration of market-oriented reforms in communist China led to the unprecedented dominance of the neoliberal model in the 1990s.

During the last decade, however, neoliberalism has come under a series of criticisms. The global economic crisis of 2008–9 is only the latest in a series of challenges to the still dominant free-market paradigm. But before we can appreciate the full magnitude of the threat facing neoliberalism, we must familiarize ourselves with its various dimensions, varieties, and policy applications. So let us commence our journey with a brief consideration of its core ideas and principles.

The three dimensions of neoliberalism

'Neoliberalism' is a rather broad and general concept referring to an economic model or 'paradigm' that rose to prominence in the 1980s. Built upon the classical liberal ideal of the self-regulating market, neoliberalism comes in several strands and variations. Perhaps the best way to conceptualize neoliberalism is to think of it as three intertwined manifestations: (1) an ideology; (2) a mode of governance; (3) a policy package. Let us carefully unpack these fundamental dimensions.

Ideologies are systems of widely shared ideas and patterned beliefs that are accepted as truth by significant groups in society. Such 'isms' serve as indispensable conceptual maps because they guide people through the complexity of their political worlds. They not only offer a more or less coherent picture of the world as it is, but also as it ought to be. In doing so, ideologies organize their core ideas into fairly simple truth-claims that encourage people to act in certain ways. These claims are assembled by codifiers of ideologies to legitimize certain political interests and to defend or challenge dominant power structures. The codifiers of neoliberalism are global power elites that include managers and executives of large transnational corporations, corporate lobbyists, influential journalists and public-relations specialists, intellectuals writing for a large public audience, celebrities and top entertainers, state bureaucrats, and politicians.

Serving as the chief advocates of neoliberalism, these individuals saturate the public discourse with idealized images of a consumerist, free-market world. Skilfully interacting with the media to sell their preferred version of a single global marketplace to the public, they portray globalizing markets in a positive light as an indispensable tool for the realization of a better world. Such market visions of globalization pervade public opinion and political choices in many parts of the world. Indeed, neoliberal decision-makers function as expert designers of an attractive ideological container for their market-friendly political agenda. Their ideological claims are laced with references to global economic interdependence rooted in the principles of free-market capitalism: global trade and financial markets, worldwide flows of goods, services, and labour, transnational corporations, offshore financial centres, and so on. For this reason, it makes sense to think of neoliberalism as a rather economistic ideology, which, not unlike its archrival Marxism, puts the production and exchange of material goods at the heart of the human experience.

The second dimension of neoliberalism refers to what the French social thinker Michel Foucault called 'governmentalities' – certain modes of governance based on particular premises, logics, and power relations. A neoliberal governmentality is rooted in entrepreneurial values such as competitiveness, self-interest, and decentralization. It celebrates individual empowerment and the devolution of central state power to smaller localized units. Such a neoliberal mode of governance adopts the self-regulating free market as *the* model for proper government. Rather than operating along more traditional lines of pursuing the public good (rather than profits) by enhancing civil society and social justice, neoliberals call for the employment of governmental technologies that are taken from the world of business and commerce: mandatory development of 'strategic plans' and 'risk-management' schemes oriented toward the creation of 'surpluses'; cost–benefit analyses and other efficiency calculations; the shrinking of political governance (so-called 'best-practice governance'); the setting of quantitative targets; the close monitoring of outcomes; the creation of highly individualized, performance-based work plans; and the introduction of 'rational choice' models that internalize and thus normalize market-oriented behaviour. Neoliberal modes of governance encourage the transformation of bureaucratic mentalities into entrepreneurial identities where government workers see themselves no longer as public servants and guardians of a qualitatively defined 'public good' but as self-interested actors

responsible to the market and contributing to the monetary
success of slimmed-down state 'enterprises'.

In the early 1980s, a novel model of public administration known
as 'new public management' took the world's state bureaucracies by
storm. Operationalizing the neoliberal mode of governance for
public servants, it redefined citizens as 'customers' or 'clients' and
encouraged administrators to cultivate an 'entrepreneurial spirit'.
If private enterprises must nurture innovation and enhance
productivity in order to survive in the competitive marketplace,
why shouldn't government workers embrace neoliberal ideals to

Neoliberalism as new public management: ten government objectives

1. Catalytic Government: Steering Rather than Rowing
2. Community-Owned Government: Empowering Rather than Serving
3. Competitive Government: Injecting Competition into Service
4. Mission-Driven Government: Transforming Rule-Driven Organizations
5. Results-Oriented Government: Funding Outcomes, Not Inputs
6. Customer-Driven Government: Meeting the Needs of the Customer, Not the Bureaucracy
7. Enterprising Government: Earning Rather than Spending
8. Anticipatory Government: Prevention Rather than Cure
9. Decentralized Government: From Hierarchy to Participation and Teamwork
10. Market-Oriented Government: Leveraging Change through the Market

Source: David Osborne and Ted Gaebler, *Reinventing Government* (1992), cited in Robert B. Denhardt, *Theories of Public Organization*, 5th edn. (Wadsworth, 2007), pp. 145–6

improve the public sector? Based on this neoliberal governmentality, US Vice-President Al Gore famously utilized new public management principles in the 1990s to subject various government agencies to a 'National Performance Review' whose declared objective was to cut 'government waste' and increase administrative efficiency, effectiveness, and accountability.

Third, neoliberalism manifests itself as a concrete set of public policies expressed in what we like to call the 'D-L-P Formula': (1) deregulation (of the economy); (2) liberalization (of trade and industry); and (3) privatization (of state-owned enterprises). Related policy measures include massive tax cuts (especially for businesses and high-income earners); reduction of social services and welfare programmes; replacing welfare with 'workfare'; use of interest rates by independent central banks to keep inflation in check (even at the risk of increasing unemployment); the downsizing of government; tax havens for domestic and foreign corporations willing to invest in designated economic zones; new commercial urban spaces shaped by market imperatives; anti-unionization drives in the name of enhancing productivity and 'labour flexibility'; removal of controls on global financial and trade flows; regional and global integration of national economies; and the creation of new political institutions, think tanks, and practices designed to reproduce the neoliberal paradigm. As we shall see in later chapters, so-called 'neoconservative' initiatives often supported the neoliberal policy agenda in pursuit of shared political objectives. In turn, many neoliberals embraced conservative values, especially 'family values', tough law enforcement, and a strong military. The nearly universal adoption of at least some parts of this policy package in the 1990s reflected the global power of the ideological claims of neoliberalism.

As we noted in the preface, the ensuing chapters of this book will pay special attention to the connection between the ideological and policy dimensions of neoliberalism by examining concrete policy applications in different settings around the world. But let us first complete our clarification of conceptual matters with a brief review of the major economic theories that fuelled the rise of neoliberalism in the late 1970s.

The intellectual origins of neoliberalism

Although neoliberalism comes in several varieties, one can find the first systematic formulation of its economic principles in the Mont Pelerin Society. Founded in 1947 by Friedrich August von Hayek, an influential member of the early 20th century Austrian School of Economics, the Society attracted like-minded intellectuals committed to strengthening the principles and practice of a 'free society' by studying the workings and virtues of market-oriented economic systems. Vowing to stem what they saw as the 'rising tide of collectivism' – be it Marxism or even less radical forms of state-centred planning – Hayek and his colleagues sought to revive classical liberalism in their attempt to challenge the dominance of Keynesian ideas. A great believer in the free market's spontaneous ability to function as a self-regulating and knowledge-generating engine of human freedom and ingenuity, Hayek considered most forms of state intervention in the economy as ominous milestones on the 'road to serfdom' leading to new forms of government-engineered despotism. His economic theory was anchored in the notion of 'undistorted price mechanisms' that were said to serve to share and synchronize local and personal knowledge, thus allowing individual members of society to achieve diverse ends without state interference. For Hayek, economic freedom could never be subordinated to political liberty and confined to the narrow sphere of material production. Rather, it was a profoundly political and moral force that shaped all other aspects of a free and open society. Surprisingly, however, the members of the Mont Pelerin Society occasionally strayed into conservative ideological territory by emphasizing the limits of human rationality and the importance of time-honoured values and traditions in the constitution of human societies.

4. Friedrich August von Hayek (1899–1992)

Libertarianism

Often associated with the economic doctrines of Friedrich von Hayek and Milton Friedman, libertarianism is a political creed hostile to government intervention. While sharing general agreement with mainstream liberalism on the primacy of individual liberty, most libertarians are strictly opposed to other liberal values such as equality, solidarity, and social responsibility. Rejecting modern governments as illegitimate for their use of 'coercive' policies, many libertarians subscribe to the utopian ideal of a loose 'society' of autonomous individuals engaged in strictly voluntary forms of exchange. Indeed, some libertarians go even so far as to demand the wholesale abolition of the state.

The neoliberal principles advocated by Hayek's Mont Pelerin Society greatly influenced the American economist Milton Friedman, winner of the 1976 Nobel Prize. The charismatic leader of the Chicago School of Economics (based at the University of Chicago), Friedman had an influential hand in guiding neoliberalism from constituting a mere minority view in the 1950s to becoming the ruling economic orthodoxy in the 1990s. Focusing on inflation as the most dangerous economic outcome of state interference – such as price controls imposed by Keynesian governments to guarantee low-income earners access to basic commodities – Friedman developed his theory of monetarism. It posited that only the self-regulating free market allowed for the right number of goods at correct prices produced by workers paid at wage levels determined by the free market. By the early 1980s, monetarists like Friedman insisted that slaying the dragon of inflation required that central banks like the US Federal Reserve pursue anti-inflationary policies that kept the supply and demand for money at equilibrium. In short, monetary policies should take precedence over fiscal policy (taxation and redistribution policies) devised by 'big government'.

5. Milton Friedman (1912–2006)

As we shall see in ensuing chapters, neoliberalism soon spread to other parts of the world – often by means of so-called 'shock therapies' devised by prominent neoliberal economists. Examples include Chile after General Augusto Pinochet's 1973 CIA-supported coup, the economic transformation of formerly communist Eastern Europe, and post-Apartheid South Africa. In some cases, domestic elites, educated in elite universities abroad, embraced neoliberalism enthusiastically. Others adopted it only grudgingly because they felt that they had no choice but to swallow the bitter pill of structural adjustment demands that inevitably accompanied much-needed IMF or World Bank loan offers. Although Chicago School economists like Friedman disliked the 1940s Keynesian regulatory framework under which the IMF

The Washington Consensus

The 'Washington Consensus' is often viewed as synonymous with 'neoliberalism'. Coined in the 1980s by the free-market economist John Williamson, the term refers to the 'lowest common denominator of policy advice' directed at mostly Latin American countries by the IMF, the World Bank, and other Washington-based international economic institutions and think tanks. In the 1990s, it became the global framework for 'proper' economic development. In exchange for much-needed loans and debt-restructuring schemes, governments in the global South were required to adhere to the Washington Consensus by following its ten-point programme:

1. A guarantee of fiscal discipline, and a curb to budget deficit
2. A reduction of public expenditure, particularly in the military and public administration
3. Tax reform, aiming at the creation of a system with a broad base and with effective enforcement
4. Financial liberalization, with interest rates determined by the market

5. Competitive exchange rates, to assist export-led growth
6. Trade liberalization, coupled with the abolition of import licensing and a reduction of tariffs
7. Promotion of foreign direct investment
8. Privatization of state enterprises, leading to efficient management and improved performance
9. Deregulation of the economy
10. Protection of property rights

and World Bank had originally been devised, their neoliberal ideological descendants in the 1990s managed to capture the upper echelons of power in these international economic institutions. With the support of the world's sole remaining superpower, they eagerly exported the 'Washington Consensus' to the rest of the world.

Let us now examine in more detail the concrete ideological and policy manifestations of neoliberalism across countries, regions, and regimes. Its various strands sometimes diverge on issues such as the precise role and appropriate size of government or take different positions on policy priorities and prescriptions. But most neoliberals share broadly similar ideological positions regarding the superiority of self-regulating market mechanisms over state intervention in producing sustained economic growth. They also agree on policies promoting individual entrepreneurial growth and productivity. Finally, they are united in their view that maintaining low levels of inflation is more important than achieving full employment. We begin our journey through the landscapes of neoliberalism by exploring two of its earliest and most spectacular strands: Reaganomics and Thatcherism.

Chapter 2
First-wave neoliberalism in the 1980s: Reaganomics and Thatcherism

The rise of neoliberalism in the English-speaking world is most notably associated with US President Ronald Reagan (1981–8) and British Prime Minister Margaret Thatcher (1979–90). Their fervent campaign to put an end to Keynesian-style 'big government' was shared by the Australian Prime Minister Malcolm Fraser (1975–83) and the Canadian Prime Minister Brian Mulroney (1984–93). These political leaders not only articulated the core ideological claims of neoliberalism but also sought to convert them into public policies and programmes. What distinguished Reagan and Thatcher from many other neoliberals, however, was their remarkable resolve to stand by their principles even when it was politically risky or inconvenient to do so. President Reagan, for example, seriously considered not running for a second term in office if doing so meant he would have to reverse his deep tax cuts. Similarly, when some conservative members within Thatcher's own Tory Party stated that they could no longer tolerate her tough anti-inflation policies, she boldly declared, 'You turn if you want to – this Lady is not for turning'. Indeed, the 'Iron Lady' was famous for coining other ideological slogans such as 'There Is No Alternative' (to her neoliberal agenda). Although the political Left in Britain lost no time in assailing such economic determinism, it nonetheless failed to assemble an alternative political vision that would prove the Prime Minister wrong.

To be sure, these examples are not meant to suggest that Reagan and Thatcher were devoid of pragmatism or that they did not make significant political compromises when deemed necessary. Nor should one assume that Mulroney and Fraser's attempts at neoliberal reform were not genuine despite their relatively vague generic policies. But what distinguished the Reagan and Thatcher *revolutions*, as they would be called, was their forceful articulation of very particular sets of neoliberal ideas and claims and their successful translation into concrete policies and programmes. Moreover, both leaders staffed their cabinets with loyal secretaries and advisers who shared their points of view. Finally, both Reagan and Thatcher sought to merge their economic neoliberalism with more traditional conservative agendas. Some commentators have even gone so far as to suggest that 'neoliberalism' and 'neoconservatism' should be used as interchangeable terms. As we shall see later in this chapter, however, such assertions appear somewhat exaggerated, for these ideologies are not identical. At the same time, however, there were significant areas of overlap between neoliberalism and neoconservatism – especially as applied to Reaganomics and Thatcherism.

Neoliberalism and neoconservatism

Contemporary neoconservatives are not 'conservative' in the classical sense, as defined by 18th-century thinkers like Edmund Burke, who expressed a fondness for aristocratic virtues, bemoaned radical social change, disliked republican principles, and distrusted progress and reason. Rather, the neoconservativism of Reagan and Thatcher resembles a muscular liberalism that is often associated with political figures like Theodore Roosevelt, Harry Truman, or Winston Churchill. In general, neoconservatives agree with neoliberals on the importance of free markets, free trade, corporate power, and elite governance. But neoconservatives are much more inclined to combine their hands-off attitude toward big business with intrusive government action for the regulation of the ordinary citizenry in the name of public security and traditional morality. Their appeals to 'law and order' sometimes drown out their concern for individual rights – albeit not for the individual as the building block of society. In foreign affairs, neoconservatives advocate an assertive and expansive use of both economic and military power, ostensibly for the purpose of promoting freedom, free markets, and democracy around the world.

By the early 1980s, many of the key members of the British Treasury who had embraced monetarism became extremely influential in shaping Thatcher's economic agenda. These included prominent Tories like Alan Budd, Terry Burns, David Laidler, Patrick Minford, and Tim Congdon. Most of them were affiliated with powerful conservative think tanks such as the Centre for Policy Studies (co-founded by Margaret Thatcher), the Institute of Economic Affairs, the Adam Smith Institute, and the Institute of Directors. Influential journalists working for the *Financial Times*, *The Times*, and *The Sunday Times* sympathetic to the Prime Minister's neoliberal agenda included William Rees-Mogg, Samuel Brittan, Bernard Levin, Peter Jay, and Ronald Butt. All of these writers were chief proponents of Thatcher's monetarist economic policy.

In the United States, outspoken neoconservatives such as Irving Kristol mobilized CEOs of some of America's wealthiest corporations to support neoliberal research institutes and think tanks such as the American Enterprise Institute, the Cato Institute, and the Heritage Foundation. They worked closely with Reagan and his staff to promote policies aimed at private-sector-led economic growth. A staunch supporter of neoliberal 'supply-side' economics, the President believed that high taxes were the prime cause of poor economic performance.

Supply-side economics and the Laffer Curve

Advocated by neoliberal economists like Arthur Laffer and embraced by President Reagan, 'supply-side economics' is based upon the assumption that long-term economic growth depends on 'freeing up' the amount of capital available for private investment. A crucial theoretical component of supply-side economics, the 'Laffer Curve' is a graphical illustration of the thesis that increases in taxation rates will not always lead to an increase in taxation revenue. As tax rates approach 100%, the curve suggests, revenue will drop as citizens will have no incentive to work harder. Supply-siders show a single-minded commitment to reducing taxes on private income. Relying on the Laffer Curve, they argue that new economic growth produced by added investment will automatically generate sufficiently large tax revenue surpluses. These, in turn, could be used by governments to pay down their debts and ultimately balance their budgets. Also known as 'trickle-down economics', supply-side economics appealed to Reagan and Republican Party legislators in the US Congress who, eager to cut taxes, were nonetheless careful to preserve politically popular social programmes like Social Security and Medicare.

Thatcher, by way of contrast, held that the growth of the money supply was the chief culprit of bad economic performance. Though cut from the same neoliberal cloth, the US President's and the Prime Minister's differing views inspired distinct policy agendas. Figure A illustrates these variations on the neoliberal theme.

Reaganomics

Immediately upon taking office in 1981, President Ronald Reagan announced his supply-side-oriented Program for Economic Recovery that was based on neoliberal principles,

Executive leader	Core neoliberal beliefs	Secondary beliefs	Core neoliberal policy issue	Secondary policy issue
Reagan (supply-sider)	Government is inefficient. Government predation leads to poor economic performance.	Monetary and fiscal stability is necessary for economic growth.	Restrict the extent of government predation through minimal taxation.	Create economic stability through deficit reduction and spending restraint.
Thatcher (monetarist)	Government is inefficient. Monetary and fiscal stability is necessary for economic growth.	Government predation leads to poor economic performance.	Create economic stability through deficit reduction and spending restraint.	Restrict the extent of predation through minimal taxation.

A. Reaganomics and Thatcherism: supply-side and monetarist neoliberalism

25

6. Ronald Wilson Reagan (1911–2004), 40th President of the United States of America (1981–9)

derided by opponents in his own party as 'Voodoo Economics'. Proclaiming to combat the toxic mixture of stagflation and high unemployment inherited from the Carter years, Reaganomics focused, first and foremost, on reducing marginal tax rates. But the President was no less determined to tackle deficit spending and existing government regulations. The only area in which

Reagan pushed strongly for spending increases was military defence, which he insisted was necessary for waging the Cold War against the Soviet 'Evil Empire' and other 'communist aggressors' around the world. We will return to the subject of foreign policy at the end of this chapter.

Although both Reagan and Thatcher saw inflation as an impediment to growth, supply-siders like the US President were keen on portraying monetarism as the 'politics of austerity'. Believing that the money supply would naturally adjust to market imperatives, Reagan did not share the Prime Minister's monetarist sense of worry over budget deficits. Lower taxes, he asserted, promoted increased growth which, in turn, would automatically generate sufficient revenues to cover existing spending for public programmes.

But when Reaganomics struggled to deliver on its promise to end deficit spending, the President's Budget Director, David Stockman, challenged this economic strategy. Stockman, a traditional fiscal conservative, publicly warned that deep tax cuts and increased military spending would make large deficits inevitable, the consequences of which could be disastrous. He therefore advised the President to further curtail funding for social programmes, including Medicare and Medicaid. Yet, Reagan did neither. Undeterred, he stayed his economic course.

Judged in the short term, Reagan's tax cuts might hardly be viewed as a neoliberal 'revolution'. From a broader perspective, however, their cumulative effect amounted to nothing less than a full-blown assault on state-led redistribution of private wealth. The Tax Reform Act of 1986, in particular, reduced the number of tax brackets to four while reducing the average individual income tax rate by about 6%. In an attempt to address mounting fears over the growing budget deficit, the Tax Reform Act raised corporate taxes to offset cuts in personal income taxes, thus seeking to make the latter 'revenue neutral'. But critics were quick to point out that Reagan's tax reforms resulted in a dramatic widening of the income gap between the middle class and the wealthy. Reagan's initial tax cuts, implemented in the early 1980s, led to a decline in government revenues that were required to cover existing spending commitments in social policy and dramatic increases in military expenditure. As a result, the administration was forced to resort to enormous levels of deficit spending to cover these revenue shortfalls.

Under intense pressure from many traditional conservatives, Reagan was eventually compelled to deal with what amounted to the largest budget deficit in US history.

His long-standing resentment against government growth paved the way for the historic enactment of what became known as the Gramm-Rudman-Hollings Deficit Reduction Initiative. Sponsored by Republican Senators Phil Gramm and Warren Rudman, the legislation fuelled intense public debate in the global North over the potential dangers of deficit spending to the American and world economy.

The Gramm-Rudman-Hollings Initiative (GRH)

Also known as the Balanced Budget and Emergency Control Act, GRH was introduced in 1985 as a method of controlling excessive government spending by the Reagan administration. It outlined spending targets that would eliminate the deficit by 1991, prompting a public debate on the dangers of the growing tendency of government to borrow and spend. A major point of contention was GRH's demand to cut social spending. Progressive members of the Democratic Party, in particular, were incensed that military spending was not subjected to the same stringent reduction schemes as social programmes. Although not all of the measures outlined in GRH were implemented, the neoliberal momentum behind it endured.

The US Federal Reserve Bank had long enjoyed relative independence in setting monetary policy, particularly with respect to interest rates. Although not at the top of his neoliberal agenda, Reagan's commitment to monetary objectives was evident in his re-appointment of Paul Volcker as Chairman of the Federal Reserve in 1983 and his subsequent appointment of the well-known monetarist Alan Greenspan in 1987. Paul Volcker launched an aggressive campaign against inflation which, by 1980, had reached into the double digits. In response, Volcker aggressively pressed for higher interest rates. By 1986, his monetarist measures had cut inflation by nearly 50%. But this reduction came at a high price for many Americans who found exorbitant interest rates on mortgages and private loans a tough medicine to swallow. Financing new homes or cars became almost impossible for low- and middle-income earners. Impatient to reap the benefits of their President's neoliberal agenda, millions of Americans initially directed their frustration at Reagan. As a result, his approval rating plummeted to just below 50% before soaring to record highs after the economy picked up in the mid-to-late 1980s.

In addition, reducing taxes and increasing military expenditure – while simultaneously trying to balance the budget – turned out to be inconsistent objectives. This was particularly evident in the area of tax policy where cuts in income taxes led to increases in corporate tax revenues. These inconsistencies helped fuel volatile exchange rates. The US dollar reached its highest point in 1980 but proceeded to fall to its lowest level during Reagan's final year in office, in 1988. What was the reason for this volatility? For one, Reagan's initial tax cuts complemented the Federal Reserve's tight monetary policy, thereby helping to create a strong dollar. Moreover, these early tax cuts encouraged international investment and spurred investor demand for US portfolio assets and treasury bonds. Subsequent increases in tax rates, particularly when levied on corporate income, however, reduced foreign investment and caused the dollar's depreciation toward the end of Reagan's second term. But the President was not particularly alarmed about this currency volatility as a weak dollar made foreign imports more expensive and American goods more desirable to both domestic and foreign consumers.

Though fiscal policy was the main focus of Reaganomics, regulatory reform was soon to follow. This effort was to be undertaken as part of Reagan's ideological commitment to 'New Federalism'. Rooted in the theories of the Public Choice School of Economics, new federalism was inspired by the neoliberal tenets of decentralization and individual choice. It regarded politics as a rational enterprise devoted to winning a maximum of votes rather than a messy strategy of governing in the public interest. Operating under the assumption that individual citizens 'vote with their feet', public choice economists argued that local governments were much better positioned to respond to individual citizens' demands because of their close proximity to their 'clients'. In other words, smaller, decentralized government was 'better' in terms of market efficiency and economic effectiveness. Moreover, new federalists saw small governments as less likely to regulate the market – hence their neoliberal slogan 'less is more'.

Reagan warmed up to the public choice/new federalist approach because it provided an appealing rationale for regulatory restraint. Believing in the value of rigorous economic statistical tools to assess policy decisions, he signed *Executive Order 12291*, which required federal agencies to utilize the methods of cost–benefit analysis in appraising government regulation proposals. Consequently, a substantial number of existing regulations were targeted for possible elimination. Moreover, the regulatory powers of government organizations like the Environmental Protection Agency (EPA) were significantly diminished. As we have seen in Chapter 1, these initiatives attest to the ability of neoliberalism to function not just as an ideology or set of polices, but also as a distinct mode of governance consistent with the principles of 'new public management' and public choice theory.

As part of his New Federalism Initiative, Reagan began to transfer federal regulatory power to the states – though often without providing them with the resources necessary for carrying out their new functions and mandates. In addition, deregulation measures were applied to key industry sectors such as communications, transportation, and banking. In one such bold move to deregulate the telecommunications industry, the administration authorized the settlement of interminable lawsuit filed by the Department of Justice against American Telephone and Telegraph (AT&T). This action resulted in the break-up of the Bell system monopoly of local telephone services into seven separate telephone companies. Under the terms of the deregulation deal, rates remained regulated but telecommunications products and services (including equipment leasing and long-distance service) were subjected to competitive market forces.

Perhaps the most controversial initiative of neoliberal Reaganomics was the deregulation of the Savings and Loans Industry (S&L). Previously, S&Ls had provided savings accounts to depositors and passed on those funds as loans in the form of home mortgages. Regarded as a relatively secure and prudent industry, S&Ls were heavily regulated while their customers' savings accounts were insured by the federal government. Claiming that S&Ls needed to be given the opportunity to compete more aggressively with other commercial banks and security markets, President Reagan's deregulation efforts allowed S&Ls to seek new forms of financing in their pursuit of higher short-term profits.

These neoliberal measures fuelled a series of mergers, acquisitions, and leverage buyouts, involving some of the nation's largest corporations. Innovative financing tools, including what came to be known as 'junk bonds', were sold to investors to finance many of these takeovers. Underperforming companies with lucrative assets, including employee pensions, were often targeted by 'corporate raiders' who initiated hostile takeovers and then sold off their assets for huge profits, usually leading to significant layoffs. Thus, speculators and stockholders thrived during the legendary Wall Street-driven Bull Market that lasted from 1984 to the autumn of 1987. Lured by the promise of quick profits and high returns, short-term investors often overlooked the substantial risks involved in such transactions. Thus, by October 1987, most stock values were seriously inflated. The disastrous correction came swiftly with the 'Black Monday' crash of the New York stock market, which lost a third of its value overnight. In the wake of this crisis, calls for the reinstatement of strict regulatory oversight grew louder. Once again, the Reagan administration turned a deaf ear to these pleas, refusing to support anti-takeover legislation on the new-federalist premise that corporate regulation was a state prerogative.

Only a few years later, rising interest rates put a drastic end to another speculation-driven phenomenon: the real estate bubble that had been expanding during the 1980s finally burst in 1991, causing the collapse of hundreds of S&Ls. The ensuing federal

7. Michael Douglas as financial tycoon Gordon Gekko in *Wall Street*: 'Greed is good'

bailout cost American taxpayers well over 100 billion dollars. The effects of this financial crisis would be felt for years. Interestingly, some of the same dynamics – the deregulation of the financial sector and the ensuing creation of a gigantic real estate bubble built on bad subprime mortgages – led to the global financial crisis of 2008–9.

Big corporate takeovers and mergers of the 1980s

1984 Lincoln First Bank/Chase Manhattan Corporation
1986 Ronald O. Perelman/Revlon
       General Electric, Incorporated/RCA
       Loew's, Incorporated/CBS
       Capital Cities, Incorporated/ABC
       Wells Fargo/Crocker National
1987 British Petroleum/Standard Oil
1988 Ames Dept. Stores/Zayre
       Philips Morris/Kraft
1989 Time-Warner/Bristol-Myers Squibb
       Kohlberg Kravis Roberts/RJR Nabisco

Expanding some early neoliberal policies of his predecessor Jimmy Carter, Reagan decided to add to the Airline Deregulation Act of 1978. Effectively eviscerating the regulatory power of the Civil Aeronautics Board, the legislation would later promote competitive bidding for route destinations. The results were mixed. On the one hand, it expanded airline services, thus boosting competition. On the other, it dramatically increased air traffic while slashing federal funding for infrastructure. Existing resources were bedraggled and air traffic controllers became overwhelmed and overworked. When the Professional Air Traffic Controllers Association protested these deteriorating work conditions and called for large-scale strikes, Reagan considered its demands 'radical' and proceeded to fire 11,000 employees. The President's drastic anti-labour measure had its intended effect: it frightened many unions into accepting the business-oriented imperatives of the new neoliberal era.

One of the most symbolically important neoliberal reforms undertaken by the Reagan administration was its attempt to privatize large portions of federally owned land. It is a relatively unknown fact that about 50% of the lands west of the Rocky Mountains are owned by the US federal government. The President argued that these lands had been 'underused' and would be managed more productively were they to be transferred into private hands. Consistent with Thatcher's neoliberal claim that the transfer of public resources to private investors meant better management and increased productivity, Reagan asserted that revenues generated from the land sales could be used for servicing the public debt. In 1983, however, the privatization scheme came to a swift and unexpected close when many federal legislators, and even officials in the executive branch, were reluctant to sell off property under their control and management. Indeed, supporters of privatization within the administration itself failed to adequately identify key constituencies in building broader legislative and administrative support for the privatization initiative. Yet, on a symbolic level, the proposed land-sale initiatives underscored the high premium that neoliberalism places on private ownership.

Furthermore, consistent with Reagan's neoliberal mode of governance, major reform initiatives were attempted in the area of social policy. Programmes and policies ranging from those aimed at the poor – such as Aid to Families with Dependent Children, school lunch programmes, and Medicaid – were increasingly dropped into the lap of the states. The use of a budgetary tool for providing federal funds to states, known as 'block grants', was significantly increased to facilitate the discreet implementation of these 'reforms'. Only major entitlement programmes, such as Social Security and Medicare, were to continue to be managed and administered by the Federal Government. However, the Reagan administration did not hesitate to subject even these popular Keynesian-era social programmes to neoliberal reforms by, for example, seeking to introduce a lean voucher system in the Medicare programme to boost 'competition' and 'efficiency' in the name of reducing public expenditures. Though the voucher experiment did not produce the results the President had expected, it served as a strong neoliberal signal for the application of market principles to the delivery of social services.

From the point of view of ardent free-trade neoliberals, Reagan's record on promoting trade policy was rather disappointing. In fact, there appears to be a wide consensus among free-traders that he was one of the more protectionist modern presidents, especially when compared to Bill Clinton and or even George W. Bush. Reagan's trade policies were often characterized by piecemeal attempts at fine-tuning and adjusting existing trade agreements pertaining to areas such as agricultural commodities and high-technology products. Supporters argue that the President's positions were linked to the interests of some of his domestic core constituencies. For example, his protectionism with respect to Japanese automobiles was specifically adopted to force East Asian countries to open their economies to US agricultural exports. Whatever the explanation for these manoeuvres might be, there is little doubt that the Reagan administration's free-trade agenda was relatively modest.

Protectionism and economic nationalism

Often portrayed as the main alternative to the free-trade ideology espoused by Adam Smith and David Ricardo, protectionism is linked to the objectives of 'economic nationalism'. One of the most influential economic nationalists of the 19th century, the German economic historian Friedrich List (1789–1846), asserted that nations, not global markets, were at the centre of commercial activity. He further argued that infant industries in the newly industrializing economies were relatively fragile and would be threatened if forced to compete under free-trade conditions with industries in the industrialized economies which already possessed capital-intensive methods of production and a skilled labour force. Thus, List proposed that newly industrializing economies adopt the use of tariffs until their infant industries were ready to compete in global markets. In the United States, protectionism and economic nationalism went for a long time hand in hand. Treasury Secretary Alexander Hamilton, for example, was a staunch economic nationalist who supported protectionism for US industries to shield them from British industrial dominance. In 1890, President Benjamin Harrison (1888–92) signed the McKinley Act which imposed tariff rates that soared to nearly 50% on imports. In 1930, President Herbert Hoover (1928–32) signed the Smoot-Hawley Act that raised tariffs in an effort to protect domestic farmers from foreign competition. More recently, former Reagan speech writer Patrick J. Buchanan and CNN TV host Lou Dobbs have become influential supporters of economic nationalism in the United States. Buchanan frequently expresses the conviction that there exists at the core of contemporary American society an irrepressible conflict between claims of American nationalism and the neoliberal imperatives of the global economy. Fearing the loss of national self-determination and the destruction of Anglo-American culture, protectionists like Buchanan see themselves as the populist leaders of a national struggle against the forces of globalization.

But, from a strong free-trade perspective, Reagan's trade legacy was somewhat redeemed in light of three crucial actions. The first was his administration's strong involvement in the 1982 GATT negotiations, which focused on liberalizing trade in the agriculture and services sectors. However, the 1982 recession ultimately compelled Reagan to cede to domestic producer demands to opt out of the discussions. The second pro-free-trade initiative was the President's active involvement in setting the agenda for a new comprehensive set of multilateral trade negotiations, known as the Uruguay Round (1986–94). Covering a range of areas from agriculture and services to intellectual property rights, the negotiations were a major force behind the ensuing free-trade trajectory of the 1990s. Third, the Reagan administration successfully negotiated the Free Trade Agreement (FTA) with Canada, which was later expanded to include Mexico. It fell to President Bill Clinton to complete this process in 1993 with the signing of the North American Free Trade Agreement (NAFTA).

Major trade organizations and agreements

In the 1980s and 1990s, the core neoliberal goal of establishing a single global market found its partial realization in major regional and international trade liberalization agreements. Leading the way forward have been many of the rich northern countries seeking to establish a single global market. GATT, for example, was successfully expanded to include nearly 120 countries. Eight rounds of negotiations ultimately resulted in tens of thousands of tariff concessions that fuelled tens of billions of dollars in international transactions. The Uruguay Round established the basis for the creation of what would later become known as the World Trade Organization (WTO) in 1995. Headquartered in Switzerland, the WTO would provide an ongoing forum for 'implementing and enforcing trade agreements, managing trade disputes, monitoring national trade policies, and providing expertise and training for its members'. US Presidents George H. W. Bush (1989–93) and Bill Clinton (1993–2001) lobbied strongly for the adoption of NAFTA. Signed in 1994, NAFTA constitutes a comprehensive set of agreements that eliminated tariffs and duties on a variety of important products, ranging from automobiles to textiles and agricultural products. It ultimately covered protections on intellectual property and sought the removal of capital controls on financial capital. Immediately upon its completion, negotiations commenced to expand NAFTA to include countries in Central America, Latin America, and the Caribbean. President George W. Bush (2001–09), in particular, championed the establishment of this Free Trade Area of the Americas (FTAA). But left-leaning Latin American leaders such as Venezuelan President Hugo Chávez, Bolivian President Evo Morales, and the Argentine President Nestor Kirchner undertook aggressive efforts to make sure that FTAA was never finalized.

Thatcherism

Deploring what she saw as a clear link between the growth of government and public spending increases, British Prime Minister Margaret Thatcher was vehemently opposed to the Keynesian credo of increasing taxes on private wealth to finance burgeoning state bureaucracies. Still, what she disliked even more was the negative effect of monetary growth on overall economic stability. Guided by this monetarist imperative, Thatcher unleashed a comprehensive set of neoliberal reforms aimed at reducing taxes, liberalizing exchange rate controls, reducing regulations, privatizing national industries, and drastically diminishing the power of labour unions.

To fight inflation, Thatcherism set rigorous, some would even say draconian, monetary growth targets. Prior to this, monetary policy was used to cover any balance of payments issues that may have

8. **Margaret Hilda Thatcher (1925–), Prime Minister of the United Kingdom (1979–90)**

ensued from increased government spending and related taxation. The perceived central importance of monetary policy was institutionalized with the adoption of the Medium Term Financial Strategy (MTFS), whose principal aim was to shift the focus of economic policy from a short-term tax-and-spend strategy to a longer-term monetary scheme. The MTFS took a comprehensive approach to economic policymaking by linking the growth of the money supply to the rising national deficit. Thus, the MTFS established a direct link between deficit spending and high interest rates. In contrast to Reagan's rather vague strategies for reducing deficit expenditure, Thatcher's MTFS contained explicit language on how these reductions should be achieved. In fact, the Prime Minister was so fixed on her monetarist objectives that she would ultimately even raise the value-added (national sales) tax and impose new taxes on North Sea oil revenues in order to reduce deficit spending – while at the same time supporting significant tax cuts on upper-income earners.

Although Thatcherism shared Reaganomics' contempt for 'big government' and large state bureaucracies, it showed little fondness for decentralization and the virtues of local government. In fact, Thatcher disliked local governing authorities, often viewing them as highly inefficient and susceptible to the corrupting influence of political patronage. For example, she made the highly controversial decision to abolish local tax rates and replace them with the infamous 'poll tax' – or 'community charge' – on a per head basis. This had the problematic effect of making fewer revenues available to local councils. Subjected to severe criticism from the public and members of her own party, the Prime Minister ultimately reversed her position.

An ardent fan of Milton Friedman's neoliberal economic theories, Thatcher was not a strong proponent of fixed exchange rates. However, in actuality, her Treasury adopted exchange rate targets that followed the German mark in the second half of the 1980s, only to withdraw from them shortly thereafter when the pound began to lose value. In 1990, she reluctantly joined the European Community's Exchange Rate Mechanism (ERM), which formally pegged the pound to the mark. But this policy faltered when German reunification fuelled inflation and drove up interest rates. Faced with the possibility of a serious economic downturn,

Thatcher's successor, John Major, withdrew from the ERM in 1992. This decision filled the coffers of shrewd currency speculators like the billionaire George Soros, who had wagered enormous sums against the British pound.

Another distinguishing feature of Thatcherism was its neoliberal privatization drive, which facilitated the sale of substantial state assets to the private sector. Privatization started in earnest in the early 1980s with the sale of the National Freight Corporation, British Aerospace, various cable and wireless services, British Rail, and Associated British Ports. It continued with the sale of Rolls-Royce Aircraft Engines, British Airports Authority, British Petroleum, British Steel, and several water and power utilities. Indeed, a significant number of state-owned industries were sold to private investors and corporations at substantially reduced prices in the hope that their new owners would upgrade their facilities in order to compete globally.

In addition, the sale of vast amounts of public housing units known as 'council houses' created a new generation of homeowners in Britain – but not without considerable social costs. Several hundred local governing councils jointly oversaw the construction and management of more than several million properties. As these councils enjoyed wide autonomy in the administration of housing resources with little or no concrete legal and procedural guidelines or accountability, Thatcher found them 'inefficient' and 'unresponsive' to tenant needs. In a daring political initiative, the Prime Minister enacted national legislation that enfranchised tenants, placing them directly into the planning process. Passed as the Housing Act of 1980, the new legislation provided existing long-term tenants with a 'right to buy' option as well as arming them with specific and binding legal rights. But many tenants who could not afford to purchase their rental units in the more appealing areas were relegated to less desirable neighbourhoods, thus exacerbating existing disparities between social groups and classes.

When confronted with massive structural unemployment stemming from deindustrialization, Thatcher called on the 'free market' to determine which jobs should be saved or cut. No doubt, she must have been aware of the fact that job losses in the manufacturing sector would directly translate into a further decline in union power. Thatcher believed that Britain's competitive advantage globally was in financial sector services, specifically centred in London. In an effort to expedite the structural shift leading to the financial rebirth of the 'City', the Prime Minister closed down coal pits, mines, and manufacturing plants when they did not meet private-sector performance standards.

London's 'Big Bang'

Under Prime Minister Margaret Thatcher, London's financial system underwent a massive neoliberal transformation. Prior to late 1986, the City's trading system was technologically outmoded and subjected to strict government rules and regulations. For example, high commissions levied on investors made it difficult for London to compete with New York, where commissions were substantially lower. Most significantly, foreign firms prepared to deal at better rates were not allowed to participate in the London stock and securities trading system. Most of these rules and exclusions were dropped literally overnight on 27 October 1986 – an event known as the 'Big Bang'. Radically deregulated by a neoliberal Prime Minister who was a firm believer in no-holds-barred competition, London quickly turned into a revitalized global financial centre. Now freely and aggressively courting large international investors, the London Stock Exchange – now upgraded to electronic, screen-based trading – became one of the most important financial markets in the world. On the down side, however, the deregulation of finance capital in Britain coincided with a massive overvaluation of stocks which contributed to the worldwide crash on 'Black Monday' (19 October 1987).

Thatcher came to realize that England's competitive advantage in the increasingly globalized 'new economy' depended on a 'flexible' and skilled workforce. The existing British employment training system, known as Active Labour Market Policy, had been run with strong union support through a pro-labour state agency called the Manpower Services Commission. The Prime Minister, however, envisioned a more neoliberal training scheme that would be more responsive to the market rather than the educational needs of unionized workers. To that end, she sought to shift the responsibility of employment from the state to the individual, arguing that well-trained and highly skilled workers would be easily employable while those with limited or outmoded skills would find themselves left behind. Ultimately, the Thatcher government would adopt an employment training scheme that diminished the role of unions in favour of a network of service-sector employers, known as Training and Enterprise Councils. This new system would lay the foundation for Thatcherism's famous 'workfare' or 'welfare to work' programme.

Considering state welfare policy to be at the heart of economic inefficiency, the Prime Minister targeted a variety of policies and programmes. Driven by her relentless quest to cut state expenditures, she sought to overhaul the child benefit provision that provided assistance to all working mothers regardless of means. Believing that such benefits should be available only to those she classified as the 'truly needy', she attempted to make the programme accessible on a strict means-tested basis. In the end, however, Thatcher abandoned her agenda after realizing that Keynesian social security and child benefit programmes had become too deeply embedded in the socio-political fabric of British society, making them politically untouchable.

Envisioning public pension reform through the same neoliberal lens through which she viewed labour market training, the Prime Minister demanded that they be 'flexible', that is, responsive to shifting market conditions. To that end, she sought to make individual employee pension accounts transferable from one job to the next. In her view, this would remove state-imposed hurdles that kept individuals from seeking higher-paying jobs with more solid futures. The plan would also 'liberate' employee accounts from traditional union pension structures, putting them in the hands of individual workers rather than unions. Once again confronted with a recalcitrant electorate still attached to the Keynesian legacy, Thatcher had to settle for more modest social reforms. Thus, she limited the bulk of her reform strategy to streamlining rules and procedures and instituting greater consistency among departments in the managing of means-testing eligibility requirements for those drawing on social benefits. At the same time, these administrative reforms were part of an attempt to change the motivational logic at the root of what she saw as bureaucratic inertia.

Indeed, both Thatcherism and Reaganomics sought to apply to the public sector neoliberal management techniques taken from the private sector. True to the principles of 'new public management', both leaders insisted that objectives were to be clearly defined and results measured and assessed strictly in relation to costs. The strategic logic behind their thinking was to target those government programmes that did not demonstrate immediate measurable benefits. This neoliberal mode of governance would prove to be fatal for many social programmes whose true benefits were observable only over the long term, and, even then, were not easily quantifiable.

However, regardless of the political party in power, expenditures on the British National Health Service (NHS) had continually increased throughout the 1970s. Thatcher rejected the idea that the problems with the NHS stemmed from funding shortages and attributed them instead to bureaucratic inefficiency. Again turning to market-based practices, she required that hospitals field competitive bids from the private sector for many services. The end of the decade of Thatcherism saw the passage of neoliberal reform legislation that gave local health authorities increased discretion and administrative powers over healthcare services – including the power

to manage costs by contracting with doctors and hospitals to
provide services.

Reaganomics and Thatcherism in foreign affairs

Reagan and Thatcher shared a pronounced neoconservative
impulse in foreign affairs which sometimes conflicted with their
neoliberal vision of establishing a single global free market.
Attached to a national imaginary that, from time to time, exploded
into hyper-patriotism, they saw themselves as the torch-bearers of
an Anglo-American civilization anchored in the ideals of political
liberty, free-market commerce, and love of country. This tension
between the national and the global imaginary expressed itself
clearly in Thatcher's chauvinistic 1982 Falklands War and
Reagan's 1983 invasion of the tiny Caribbean island of Grenada. To
be sure, decades of Cold War hostility and mistrust between the
capitalist West and communist East only intensified Reagan's and
Thatcher's desire to stand up to the 'Evil Empire'. In this respect,
both leaders showed a remarkably 'un-neoliberal' eagerness to
utilize the state and its financial resources in their struggle against
the Soviet Union and its satellites and dependencies around the
world. Rather than confronting the USSR with direct military
action – as feared by the political Left in the early days of the
Reagan administration – the American President dramatically
increased military spending in his risky effort to force the Soviets
to compete in an intensive arms race they could ill afford.

The 1982 Falklands War

In 1982, Margaret Thatcher decided to go to war with Argentina
over a territorial dispute involving the Falklands (Malvinas)
occupied by Britain. Indeed, the two countries had been
embroiled in a long-standing disagreement over the sovereign
control of this tiny group of islands in the South Atlantic. When

Argentina's military government ordered several thousand troops to occupy the islands, Thatcher responded by launching a formidable naval assault to recover them. The Prime Minister's bellicose response suggested that her neoconservative impulses had overwhelmed her professed neoliberal approach to policymaking. After all, neoliberal prescriptions would have encouraged the pursuit of a coordinated diplomatic initiative launched through international channels prior to direct military involvement. After two months of fighting, resulting in the loss of about 600 Argentine and 200 British forces, Argentina conceded a humiliating defeat that would ultimately bring down the country's military regime. It fell to the newly elected neoliberal President Carlos Menem (1989–99) to normalize relations with Britain in 1990, when the two countries agreed to shelve the issue of the Falklands sovereignty and instead focus on advancing Argentina's neoliberal economic agenda. In 1991, these efforts contributed to the formation of Mercosur (Southern Common Market), a South American regional free-trade agreement.

Perhaps in response to this strategy, the Communist Party's Politburo elected in 1985 a political reformer who had built a reputation as a dynamic and competent 'ideas man'. Ironically, Mikhail Gorbachev also showed some neoliberal tendencies in his efforts to spearhead modest market-oriented reforms 'from within'. Retaining a healthy scepticism as to the ultimate objectives of the new Soviet leader, Reagan and Thatcher gradually warmed up to the charismatic Secretary General. They publicly endorsed both Gorbachev's cultural revolution of *glasnost* (openness about public affairs) and his comprehensive economic and political restructuring programme, known as *perestroika*. Impressed by the Russian leader's willingness to consider market-oriented reforms, his Western counterparts recognized that they could work with him to build a new relationship based on largely neoliberal ideals.

The first results of this ideological rapprochement were evident in a series of breakthroughs in arms-control agreements.

As everyone knows, Gorbachev's reforms ultimately led to the unravelling of the Soviet Union and the political independence of its Eastern European client states. But it is difficult to gauge the precise extent to which the demise of communism was fuelled by neoliberalism. After all, the Soviet Union had long suffered from severe structural deficiencies. By the time Gorbachev took the reins of power, the country was overwhelmed by intractable economic stagnation, perennial shortages of essential consumer goods, staggering waste, bureaucratic inefficiency, and the Communist Party's declining political legitimacy. Reagan's muscular foreign policy, supported by excessive military spending, merely added to the Kremlin's problems. Still, there is very little doubt that neoliberal pioneers like Reagan and Thatcher recognized the historic opportunity presented by Gorbachev's new ideological outlook. The rapid decline and astonishing collapse of the Soviet Empire ultimately served to confirm and validate their own beliefs about the superiority of free markets and their liberal-democratic political systems.

As shown in Chapter 1, first-wave neoliberalism in the 1980s was interlaced with the geopolitical imperative to stop the spread of communism and socialist developmentalism in the Third World. Reagan, as we noted in the case of Grenada, intervened in regional conflicts, openly or covertly supporting guerrilla movements to overthrow Soviet-sponsored regimes based on their supposed 'ideological threat' to the US and its allies. The President came to understand that the most devastating blows against the USSR were dealt by his support of counter-revolutionary movements enjoying Soviet aid in different parts of the world. Two more examples of this strategy were Reagan's effort to topple the socialist Sandinista government in Nicaragua and his response to the Soviet invasion of Afghanistan. Here, rather than confronting the Soviets head on, Reagan ordered a steady stream of arms

9. Reagan and Gorbachev shaking hands at their 1988 summit in Moscow after exchanging ratifications of the Intermediate Nuclear Force Treaty

shipments to Afghanistan in support of their opponents, the Islamist 'freedom fighters' (*mujahideen*). Preoccupied with deepening economic problems at home, the Soviet regime found it impossible to continue spending 40% of its annual budget to fund their Afghan War. Eventually, the Soviets were forced to withdraw and Reagan claimed victory. Fought on openly ideological grounds, these proxy wars in the global South were carefully selected to prove the superiority of free-market capitalism to the rest of the world.

Conclusion

First-wave neoliberalism in the 1980s amounted to a successful ideological crusade against Keynesian-style 'big government' and state 'interference' in the market. Anchored in common principles centred on releasing the entrepreneurial energies of the individual, Reaganomics and Thatcherism nonetheless represented quite unique responses to an increasingly globalized economic and political context. As we have seen in this chapter, these two variations on the neoliberal theme took distinct approaches to issues such as the relative importance accorded to budget deficits and taxes. Both advocated a reduced role of government, but their economic initiatives depended, paradoxically, on the muscle of state imposed neoliberal reforms on local and regional authorities. Thus, it is important to recognize that the rise of neoliberalism would have been impossible without strong government action. Similarly, while espousing the need to cut public expenditures for social programmes, Reaganomics and Thatcherism supported increases in military spending. In spite of their ideological tensions and contradictions, however, it would be foolish not to acknowledge the broad appeal enjoyed by these two variants of neoliberalism by the late 1980s. It is a remarkable testimony to the power of Reaganomics and Thatcherism that the forces of the democratic Left started to incorporate major portions of the neoliberal agenda into their own political programmes.

Chapter 3

Second-wave neoliberalism in the 1990s: Clinton's market globalism and Blair's Third Way

The ideological positions adopted by President Bill Clinton and Prime Minister Tony Blair in the 1990s reflect a middle-of-the-road approach that embraced major portions of neoliberalism while also seeking to incorporate parts of a socially progressive agenda traditionally associated with political parties of the democratic Left. Hoping to broaden the appeal of his 'reformed' party to all social classes, Blair argued that 'New Labour' stood for 'social advancement through individual achievement'. This slogan was meant to convey that the pursuit of private-sector-led economic growth could be successfully combined with the government's responsibility to provide a reliable level of social services to all its citizens. For example, at a 1998 policy seminar in Washington, DC, the energetic Prime Minister announced his intention to create a global network of 'centre-left' parties that would develop a joint policy framework capable of responding to the challenges of the post-Cold War world. The key to forging such a 'Third Way' beyond the time-worn agendas of the old Keynesian Left and the new Thatcherist Right, Blair insisted, was a commitment to the centre-left principle of strengthening social solidarity without dropping the neoliberal ideal of market-oriented entrepreneurship.

Similarly, when President Clinton famously announced to Congress and the American people in his 1996 State of the Union Address that 'the era of big government is over', he did not intend to imply that there was no place in the global age for trimmed-down, activist governments operating more efficiently by embracing a neoliberal mode of governance. Like his British counterpart, the American President was confident that what some neoliberal enthusiasts called 'super-capitalism' or 'turbo-capitalism' could be combined with moderate social welfare provisions and greater corporate responsibility. Moreover, both leaders agreed on the necessity of ridding first-wave neoliberalism of its neoconservative accretions – hyperpatriotism and militarism, attachment to antiquated 'family values', disdain for multiculturalism, and neglect of ecological issues. They hoped that their 'purified' product – a socially conscious market globalism – would propel the entire world toward a new golden age of technological progress and prosperity. Such 'modernized' second-wave neoliberalism had a tremendous impact on the political landscape of the post-communist 1990s, for it represented an attractive model for progressive political forces hungry to return to power after more than a decade of Reaganomics and Thatcherism. By the turn of the century, the leaders of traditional social-democratic European parties – Dutch Prime Minister Wim Kok, Italian Prime Ministers Romano Prodi and Massimo D'Alema, French Prime Ministers Pierre Beregovoy and Lionel Jospin, and German Chancellor Gerhard Schröder – had embraced the new left-centre agenda. United in their attempts to liberalize trade relations and integrate national economies into a single global market, Clinton and Blair would eventually take the credit for the 'Roaring Nineties' – a decade of economic boom.

Bill Clinton's market globalism

From the very outset of his presidency, Bill Clinton was convinced that the American economy was inextricably linked to a set of processes that made the world a far more interconnected and

10. **President Bill Clinton and British Prime Minister Tony Blair in conversation at 'Roundtable Discussion on the Third Way: Progressive Governance for the 21st Century', held on 25 April 1999 in Washington, DC**

interdependent place. A 'new economy' of global reach was rapidly evolving, seemingly driven by irresistible market forces. Emerging as *the* buzzword of the 1990s, 'globalization' was used to refer primarily to the extension and intensification of *economic* relations across the planet. To be sure, economics were a big part of the globalization story, for gigantic compression of time and space would have been impossible without the worldwide expansion of markets, the rise of transnational corporations (TNCs), and the intensification of economic flows across the globe. Moreover, these economic developments were facilitated by the rapid transformation of information, communication, and transportation technology – a 'digital revolution' epitomized by the proliferation of personal computers, the Internet, satellite TV, standardized containers, fibre-optic cables, electronic barcodes, and global supply chains. But globalization unfolded not merely on the material plane of commerce and technology. It was also a direct consequence of the worldwide dominance of neoliberal ideology following the 1989–91 collapse of Soviet communism. The public interpretation of globalization as a mostly economic phenomenon driven by the irreversible dynamics of the free market and cutting-edge technology was encouraged by executives of large transnational corporations, corporate lobbyists, prominent journalists and public-relations specialists, cultural elites and entertainment celebrities – and political leaders like Bill Clinton who articulated their neoliberal agenda within such a 'globalist' framework.

As we discussed in Chapter 1, these global power elites imbued 'globalization' with neoliberal ideas and meanings, and thus pushed their influential ideological narrative of 'market globalism' across national and cultural boundaries. For example, one of these neoliberal claims presents the creation of globally integrating markets as a rational process that furthers individual freedom and material progress in the world. The underlying assumption here is that markets and consumerist principles are universally applicable because they appeal to all (self-interested) human beings regardless of their social context. Not even stark cultural differences should be seen as obstacles in the establishment of a single global free market in goods, services, and capital. A related neoliberal claim states that the liberalization of trade and the global integration of markets will ultimately benefit all people materially. This assertion is designed to enhance the global appeal of neoliberalism because it seeks to assure people that the creation of a single global market will lift entire regions out of poverty. Indeed, international economic organizations like the IMF and the World Bank justified their imposition of structural adjustment programmes on less-developed countries in terms of 'poverty alleviation'.

Another neoliberal claim portrays the liberalization and global integration of markets as inevitable and irreversible, almost like some natural force such as the weather or gravity. This assertion makes it easier for neoliberals to convince people that they must adapt to the inherent rules of the free market if they are to survive and prosper. Still another claim links the notion of globally expanding, self-regulating markets to the idea of democracy and individual choice, suggesting that economic and political forms of freedom are intricately connected. At the same time, however, neoliberals insist on the primacy of markets over politics by arguing that the establishment of democracy depends upon free-market economics, and not the other way around.

The five claims of market globalism

Claim 1: Globalization is about the liberalization and global integration of markets.

Claim 2: Globalization is inevitable and irresistible.

Claim 3: Nobody is in charge of globalization.

Claim 4: Globalization benefits everyone (in the long run...).

Claim 5: Globalization furthers the spread of democracy and freedom in the world.

A convinced 'market globalist', President Clinton believed that a sustained expansion of the US economy depended on the economic vitality of the global economy. Seeing enormous possibilities for mutual growth that would accompany furthering trade ties with the so-called 'emerging economies' of the global South, the President viewed trade as the prime vehicle of his economic approach. This is not to say that Clinton operated completely outside a national framework. America would remain the leader of the world, he insisted, but it would exert its influence primarily through the use of 'soft power' rather than 'hard power'. Thus, he envisioned a world connected through trade relationships designed to serve America's interests as well as complement old military-based alliances like NATO. This strategy was Clinton's version of the traditional liberal claim that commercially interdependent countries were less likely to go to war.

Hard power and soft power

Coined by Joseph Nye Jr, an international relations expert and former Clinton administration official, these concepts have become stock-in-trade terms in the contemporary discourse of international relations. Hard power refers to military and economic might that gets other nations or political players to change their positions. It rests on inducements and threats ('carrots' and 'sticks'). Soft power, on the other hand, refers to the use of cultural and ideological appeals to effect their desired outcomes without commanding allegiance. It relies on attraction and seduction much more than on crude force. In recent US foreign policy, soft power has been associated with the neoliberal multilateralism of President Bill Clinton, whereas hard power is usually linked to the neoconservative unilateralism of President George W. Bush.

As described in a best-selling book on the Roaring Nineties authored by Joseph Stiglitz, economic advisor in the Clinton administration and former chief economist of the World Bank, market globalism was based on the neoliberal thesis that free trade would bring unprecedented prosperity to both the developed and developing world. Although the President always maintained that government policies and programmes had their place when free markets destabilized existing social networks, his administration nonetheless sought to impose on developing countries radical market-oriented 'structural adjustment programmes' through international economic institutions like the IMF or the World Bank. In spite of American claims that such trade policies were meant for the benefit of the entire global community of nations, Clinton's market globalism was not about promoting 'genuine multilateral agreements or providing a forum for an open dialogue of alternative views'. Rather, it was designed to perpetuate US hegemony.

The same can be said about Clinton's grand strategy of promoting NAFTA and the GATT Uruguay Trade Round negotiations, initiated by his Republican predecessors and signed by him in 1994 in Marrakech, Morocco. The treaty allowed for a tightening of the neoliberal rules governing the international economic system and established the powerful WTO in the place of the old GATT. It further reduced trade barriers on goods, expanded trade liberalization of services, provided clarification of what counted as 'unfair trade' practices, and promoted an international agreement on intellectual property rights (TRIPs). Clinton made sure that these new provisions – especially the liberalization of the service industry and intellectual property rights (where the US enjoyed a major comparative advantage) – became the cornerstone of the Marrakech Agreement. At the same time, however, it should be noted that Clinton understood that neoliberal policies promoting competitive markets through free trade had to be balanced against concerns related to social and environmental justice. To these ends, he sought to strengthen his executive power to negotiate amendments on matters covering international labour and environmental standards. We will explore in more detail the impact of this neoliberal trade agenda on the global South in the next two chapters.

But nowhere were Clinton's efforts of exporting the neoliberal Washington Consensus to the rest of the world more visible than in his economic strategy regarding the successor states of the former Soviet Union. Based on his strong relationship with the increasingly problematic Russian President Boris Yeltsin, Clinton managed to insert into the country dozens of American economic 'advisors' to direct Russia's economic transition from communism to capitalism. In addition, the US President supported the G-7 and the IMF in their drastic recommendations to impose the sort of 'shock therapy' on Russia that had been previously employed with mixed results in Poland at the advice of American experts led by Harvard economist Jeffrey Sachs. By the mid-1990s, Sachs had emerged as Yeltsin's chief economic advisor, urging him and his rather autocratic inner political circle to persevere with the 'big bang' approach to the economic transition that demanded the lifting of price controls, the privatization of nearly 250,000 state-owned companies, and the liberalization of trade. The reward for staying the course was to be the continuation of massive loans from the IMF and other international economic institutions.

Toward the end of the 1990s, the dire consequences of the shock therapy in Russia became obvious in a dramatic widening of economic inequality. A tiny power elite known as the 'oligarchs' reaped almost all of the benefits. But President Clinton was so convinced of the merits of these neoliberal reforms – and certain that the Yeltsin government was the most reliable agent to carry out them out – that he was willing to turn a blind eye to the Russian President's increasingly authoritarian actions, including the dissolution of Parliament, the suspension of the Constitutional Court, pervasive censorship, and the escalation of the conflict in Chechnya into a full-blown war. As a result of the 1997–8 Asian financial crisis, Russia suffered a sharp decline in its earnings from oil and other resource exports. Foreign investors swiftly withdrew the capital from Russian markets, causing serious inflation and a breakdown of the country's banking system. The Yeltsin government was forced to devalue the ruble and stop payment on $40 billion in ruble bonds. Although the economy eventually recovered from this crisis, the blows to Russian democracy proved to be permanent, and the country remains in the rule of 'oligarchs', as reflected in the eight years of Vladimir Putin's presidency and continuing leadership.

On the domestic front, Clinton's market globalism was focused on returning the US economy to its former glory. The 1991 recession following the S&L crisis discussed in Chapter 2 had plunged the

Second-wave neoliberalism in the 1990s

nation into a severe fiscal crisis. Already approaching $150 billion during the last years of the Reagan presidency, the annual budget deficit eventually climbed to nearly $300 billion in the early 1990s. In a desperate effort to reverse this dangerous dynamic, President George H. W. Bush made the controversial decision in 1990 to raise taxes on upper-income earners, thereby violating a core tenet of Reaganomics. It was in the wake of this decision that presidential candidate Bill Clinton started listening to advisors urging that reduction of the budget deficit be moved to the centre of his economic agenda. Excessive levels of public borrowing, they reasoned, would deter private investors. Clinton's economic advisors also pointed to the negative effect of high long-term interest rates, arguing that the best way to bring these down was to control the growth of the federal deficit.

When he assumed office in January 1993, President Clinton lost little time in committing his administration to this neoliberal economic drive toward fiscal stability. Indeed, his large economic team was led by so-called 'deficit hawks' with strong ties to Wall Street such as Alice Rivlin, Lloyd Bentsen, Robert Rubin, Lawrence Summers, and Leon Panetta. Moreover, Clinton sought the advice of Federal Reserve Chairman Alan Greenspan, who reinforced his conviction that a massive federal deficit reduction plan of 500 billion dollars over five years was economically feasible. Mindful of the potential effects that government expenditures might have on rising inflation, the President not only established draconian spending limits consistent with Greenspan's recommendations but also set an ambitious inflation target of 3% to 3.5%. In a calculated effort to provide further comfort to nervous investors, he offered unqualified discretion to Greenspan and the independent authority of the Federal Reserve Bank regarding monetary policy and the setting of interest rates. Thus publicly signalling his unwillingness to influence Federal Reserve policy for political purposes, the centre-left President broke with the practices of his

Republican predecessor George H. W. Bush, who, in the depth of the 1991 recession, had pressured Greenspan to lower interest rates and boost the economy just before the 1992 election.

By the mid-1990s, this combination of neoliberal fiscal and monetary policies began having a positive effect. The budget deficit declined and long-term interest rates fell – without weakening the dollar or overheating the economy. As a result, the US attracted new international investment from East Asia, the stocks of American high-tech companies skyrocketed, and Silicon Valley experienced an unprecedented boom. During that period, a number of Asian and Latin American countries adopted fixed exchange rates that were pegged to the stable US dollar, making it more attractive for those nations to buy US bonds and other assets. Flush with cash, Americans consumed like never before, targeting, in particular, big-ticket items like computers, appliances, automobiles, and real estate. At the same time, however, this new-found prosperity resulted in political pressure to reduce taxes as voices echoing the principles of Reaganomics grew louder.

But rather than offering tax relief to high-income earners as Reagan had done, Clinton's tax cuts were aimed at capital gains investments made by homeowners in real property, and securities and stocks, as well as businesses investing in new research and development in high-technology sectors. Consistent with second-wave neoliberal goals of blending market initiatives with social concerns, the administration argued that tax breaks for American venture capitalists and start-up companies would encourage breakthroughs in technology and medical research that would ultimately benefit the entire global community. The 1997 Federal Budget, for example, included more than 10 billion dollars of business and capital gains tax relief over five years. A year later, the President signed a massive tax cut package totalling nearly $100 billion that provided further relief for capital gains and estate taxes, while also providing limited tax relief for working families earning less than $100,000 a year. But these tax cuts also benefited some powerful US corporations, such as Hewlett-Packard, Johnson and Johnson, and Microsoft. The compensation packages of American CEOs soared to new heights during the 1990s, while wages stagnated or grew only marginally. Indeed, the 2000 National Census Data would reveal a dramatic widening of economic disparities in America.

But perhaps the most radical neoliberal measures of the Clinton administration related to the further deregulation of the economy. Arguing that 'antiquated regulatory policies' were curtailing entrepreneurial initiatives aided by technological breakthroughs in telecommunications and the development of new international financial instruments, Clinton undertook some of the most comprehensive deregulatory reforms of the 20th century. For example, the Financial Services Modernization Act of 1999 removed the legal divisions between commercial and investment banking as well as those between insurance companies and brokerage houses, thus scrapping one of the major Keynesian regulations of Franklin Delano Roosevelt's New Deal. The potential dangers of such profound deregulations of the finance sector would not become fully apparent until the global financial crisis of 2008–9. Other deregulatory measures paved the way for an avalanche of mergers in the telecommunications industry, rivalling the break-up of AT&T initiated by the Reagan administration a decade earlier. Clinton's Telecommunications Act of 1996, for example, led to spectacular mega-mergers, including those involving SBC-Pacific Bell-Ameritech, Bell Atlantic-Nynex-GTE, Quest US West, AOL-Time Warner, AT&T-TCI, and the now defunct World-MCI. Overturning several key regulatory measures adopted previously under the 1992 Cable Act, the 1996 law allowed local Bell companies to compete in long-distance services and cable TV delivery. The Clinton

		1996 Salary and Bonus	Long-term compensation	Total Pay
1	Lawrence Coss, Green Tree Financial	102,499	None	102,499
2	Andrew Grove, Intel	3,003	94,587	97,590
3	Sanford Weill, Travelers Group	6,330	87,828	94,157
4	Theodore Waitt, Gateway 2000	965	80,361	81,326
5	Anthony O'Reilly, H. J. Heinz	2,736	61,500	64,236
6	Sterling Williams, Sterling Software	1,448	56,801	58,249
7	John Reed, Citicorp	3,467	40,143	43,610
8	Stephen Hilbert, Conseco	13,962	23,450	37,732
9	Casey Cowell, U.S. Robotics	3,430	30,522	33,952
10	James Moffett, Freeport-McMoran C&G	6,956	26,776	33,732
11	John Chambers, Cisco Systems	619	32,594	33,213
12	Stephen Wiggins, Oxford Health Plans	1,738	27,270	29,008
13	Eckhard Pfieffer, Compaq Computer	4,250	23,546	27,796
14	Stephen Case, America Online	200	27,439	27,639
15	John Welch, General Electric	6,300	21,321	27,621
16	Richard Scrushy, Healthsouth	11,380	16,197	27,577
17	Henry Silverman, HFS	3,752	19,990	23,742
18	Norman Augustine, Lockheed Martin	2,781	20,324	23,105
19	John Amerman, Mattel	3,732	18,923	22,655
20	Drew Lewis, Union Pacific	3,131	18,320	21,452

B. The best-paid US CEOs, 1996 (in $000)

Source: Business Week, 21 April 1997

The years of controlled (regulated) capitalism	
1950	5.34
1955	6.15
1960	6.79
1965	7.52
1970	8.03
1975	8.12
The years of deregulation and turbo-capitalism	
1980	7.78
1985	7.77
1990	752
1992	7.41
1994	7.41
1996	7.50
1997	7.66

C. Average hourly earnings of non-supervisory employees in private, non-farm employment, 1950–97 (in constant 1982 US$)

Source: Edward Luttwak, *Turbo-Capitalism*, p. 96

administration claimed that such deregulation would stimulate vibrant competition and expand service options for consumers at improved rates. But various consumer groups – and even conservative economists – argued that the overall effects of the Telecommunications Act would result in steep increases in service fees and a marked tendency toward the formation of local and regional corporate monopolies.

However, the Clinton administration countered such allegations by pointing to its steadfast commitment to undercutting monopolies by encouraging rigorous competition. Indeed, the

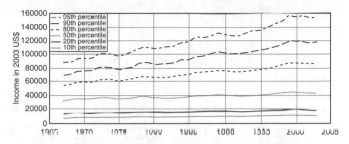

D. Household shares of aggregate income in the US, 1967–2003

Source: US Census Bureau <http://www.census.gov>

President supported vigorous anti-trust campaigns involving high-profile government lawsuits against Microsoft, Intel Corp, and American Airlines. In its case against Microsoft, the Department of Justice alleged that the software giant – which held a virtual monopoly over desktop computer operating systems – had deliberately attempted to squelch competition by requiring major computer manufacturers to include its own Microsoft Explorer Internet web browser package along with its entire Windows 95 operating system software. Under these conditions, software companies like Netscape, which produced their own web browsers, would be unable to compete on a level playing field. In the case of Intel Corporation, the Federal Trade Commission alleged that the company had withheld vital intellectual property, thereby depriving their customers of vital information regarding Intel microprocessors. In the case against American Airlines, the Department of Justice claimed that the carrier had engaged in 'predatory pricing' when it reduced the cost of flights to and from one of its hubs in a deliberate attempt to obstruct competition from other airlines seeking to use the same facility. Although Microsoft and Intel lost their cases, critics complained that they were given largely symbolic fines that failed to change a business environment skewed in their favour. From Clinton's neoliberal perspective, however, these cases reflected his administration's strong commitment to defend the free market and encourage competition.

Given market globalism's pronounced neoliberal sympathies in the areas of trade and fiscal policy, we should perhaps turn toward social policy to ascertain what, if anything, remained of the political agenda of the traditional Left. It is worth noting that Clinton steadfastly maintained that his pro-business policies were intricately interwoven with progressive social programmes. And yet, his critics on the Left have singled out his attempts to replace 'welfare as we know it' as evidence for his neoliberal extremism. It is, indeed, true that the roots of Clinton's 'welfare-to-work' philosophy were firmly planted in Ronald Reagan's Family Support Act of 1988. Then serving as the Governor of Arkansas, Clinton strongly supported a programme known as 'workfare' in his home state. Presenting it as a successful marriage between labour skill development and public assistance for the unemployed, he argued that it would support the poor without subjecting them to 'welfare dependency'. Indeed, Clinton's neoliberal ideas on social policy stemmed from his affiliation with a rising party faction known as the 'New Democrats'. The group included other prominent 'centrists' such as Al Gore, Dave McCurdy, Ed Kilgore, and Joseph Lieberman who connected to the newly formed Democratic Leadership Council, which embraced the neoliberal principles of 'individual responsibility'

The Democratic Leadership Council (DLC)

Founded in 1985, the DLC emerged as the founding organization of the New Democrats in the United States. Its declared mission is to promote debate within the Democratic Party and the general public about political and economic issues. Adopting a neoliberal 'pragmatism' in response to the emerging challenges of the New Economy, the DLC emphasizes three core principles: (1) Promoting opportunity for all; (2) Demanding responsibility from everyone; (3) Fostering a new sense of community. Closely associated with the DLC, Bill Clinton managed to move his party toward the political centre during the eight years of his presidency.

and 'accountability' in place of the old Left's credo of 'collective welfare'.

In 1996, President Clinton signed the Welfare Reform Act, which replaced the federal programme of Aid to Dependent Children, founded in 1935 as part of FDR's Social Security Act. The Clinton administration's version of 'welfare' now required work in exchange for assistance. A maximum of two years of benefits were delivered before parents were compelled to work or engage in job (re)training. No recipient was permitted more than five years of cumulative assistance. However, there were a number of special considerations, which included provisions for childcare and medical insurance for short-term unemployed mothers. Mandating a reduction of allocations and limiting the duration of the welfare payments, the 1996 Act also made it virtually impossible for single mothers to attend school full-time or part-time in order to increase their skills and qualify for better jobs. As a result, welfare recipients were often forced to accept short-term, low-paying work in the service sector.

Consistent with Reagan's approach to 're-inventing government' by adopting a neoliberal mode of governance that measured success primarily in terms of efficiency and profitability, Clinton supported initiatives for contracting out to private-sector companies many public services administered by county and municipal authorities. Critics claimed that this severely complicated the delivery of services such as federally mandated oversight of worker compliance and childcare for single-income mothers. They argued that the President seemed to overlook the fact that successful implementation of these policies would require complex coordination among various agencies within the different levels of government and the private sector that was often difficult to achieve. Still, it must be noted that the Clinton administration supported several important centre-left programmes such as increases in the federal minimum wage as well as an Earned Income Tax Credit designed to provide economic assistance to America's working poor. Along with his partner, Hillary Clinton, the

What's 'Left' of Clinton's social agenda?

- A Patient's Bill of Rights, which, among other things, allowed workers to keep their health coverage (provided they could afford it) when they transitioned between jobs and allowed them to keep their doctors when they changed employers;

- A Family Medical Leave initiative that allowed employees to take some time off to care for a sick family member or a newborn without fear of losing their jobs;

- Streamlined rules and requirements governing student loans that provided higher lending limits to borrowers in order to make college education accessible to workers requiring new job skills in an increasingly complex global economy.

current US Secretary of State, the President put strong efforts into an ultimately unsuccessful universal healthcare initiative that would have covered over 40 million uninsured working Americans.

Tony Blair's Third Way

In the wake of Tony Blair's decisive 1997 electoral triumph, Anthony Giddens, then Director of the London School of Economics and one of Blair's trusted advisors, suggested that the new government would forge a 'Third Way' sensitive to the challenges posed by the New Economy in the dawning global

Anthony Giddens on the Third Way

The Third Way involves a balance between regulation and deregulation, on transnational as well as national and local levels; and a balance between the economic and non-economic life of the society. The second of these is at least as important as the first, but attained in some part through it.

Source: Anthony Giddens, *The Third Way* (Cambridge: Polity Press, 1998), p. 100

age. This new approach, Giddens explained, would not only transcend the vexing political dualisms of the past but also bridge the stark divide between free-market dynamics and concerns for the public good.

Unveiling his Third Way, Tony Blair indeed promised the British people to put an end to the old politics of 'class warfare'. Seeking to reconcile middle-class concerns with business interests, the charismatic Prime Minister proceeded to use his considerable political skills to forge new coalitions and bipartisan networks that brought together individuals and groups from a broad ideological spectrum. Blair's drive to the political centre was a direct consequence of the low political appeal of the Labour Party during the decade of Thatcherism. Their long absence from political power awakened a new generation of Labour leaders inspired by Tony Blair and Gordon Brown who embraced the power of neoliberal ideas to fundamentally change the relationship between government and the marketplace. Convinced that controlling government growth and expenditures rather than redistributing national wealth was the best means of attaining prosperity and promoting employment, Blair and Brown signalled the abandonment of their party's socialist heritage in order to broaden its political base under the 'New Labour' brand.

Undoubtedly, this shift toward neoliberalism was inspired by the electoral success of Bill Clinton and the New Democrats, for, in the autumn of 1997, top-level representatives of the Clinton administration led by then Deputy Treasury Secretary Larry Summers and First Lady Hillary Clinton joined with members of the newly elected Blair government to discuss economic policy. Blair's Third-Way 'modernizers', as they called themselves at the time, readily embraced the basic principles of Clinton's market globalism. Following this meeting, the neoliberal New Labour government immediately sought to build credibility with the business community by emphasizing the values of individual ownership and entrepreneurship. Consistent with neoliberal values, the Prime Minister argued that remaining social inequalities could best be tackled by fundamentally changing the 'paternalistic' relationship between state and society to one based on a 'social partnership' among individuals.

Like Clinton's market globalism, the Third Way emphasized the importance of global cooperation and consensus-building through international institutions. Hence, Blair's strong sympathies for the ongoing process of European integration. Indeed, the new Prime Minister's pro-EU sentiments contrasted markedly with those of his Conservative predecessors. Initially, Blair had great hopes for British participation in the single-currency European Monetary Union as outlined in the 1992 Maastricht Treaty. Thus, he directed the Treasury to set up several 'Euro forums' spearheaded by renowned business leaders who had already been working for convergence at the regional level. In addition, the government enacted customs reforms that enabled British firms to pay taxes, issue shares, and receive certain grants in the new currency. Warning that his country could no longer afford to pretend that the Euro did not exist, Blair was convinced that Euro membership would spell enormous opportunities for British business and financial markets courting new investments that would otherwise have remained outside the 'Eurozone'.

But Blair's attitude dramatically changed when the economic performance of the Eurozone did not seem to meet his high expectations. While his New Labour government had drastically limited public spending, a number of other countries, including Germany and France, had well exceeded the deficit spending limits outlined in the Maastricht Treaty. From Blair's perspective, therefore, the stability and growth strategy contained in the Treaty had lost much credibility. Increasingly reluctant to abandon the stable British pound for the seemingly tenuous and fluctuating Euro, the Prime Minister eventually resolved to remain outside the Eurozone. In the short term, his decision was vindicated by the fact that foreign direct investment in Britain rose from $20 billion per year in the mid-1990s to more than $80 billion in 2001, whereas France and Germany enjoyed only moderate growth rates.

Echoing the principles of Clinton's market globalism, Blair argued that Britain would only enhance its global competitiveness by

Maastricht Treaty's convergence criteria

Here are the treaty's five criteria that national economies had to meet in order to be eligible to join the Eurozone:

- A nation's annual budget deficit has to be below 3% of GDP.
- A nation's public debt has to be less than 60% of GDP (the public debt is the cumulative total of annual budget deficits).
- A nation should have an inflation rate within 1.5% of the three EU countries with the lowest rate.
- Long-term interest rates must be within 2% of the three lowest interest rates in the EU.
- Exchange rates must be kept within moderate fluctuation margins of Europe's exchange-rate mechanism.

Source: BBC News, Monday, 30 April 2001

adopting a coherent macroeconomic framework for taxation and spending practices. In a deliberate effort to reassure investors that he was committed to managing the coffers of the state according to a neoliberal mode of governance, Blair adopted a Code for Fiscal Stability, which institutionalized the five principles of prudent fiscal management: transparency, stability, responsibility, fairness, and efficiency. Moreover, the Code required that the Prime Minister and his government adhere to clearly stated objectives and rules that had to be reported to and discussed with the business community. This rules-based approach to fiscal policy eventually led to the introduction of periodical Comprehensive Spending Reviews that outlined departmental spending plans and objectives according to strict cost–benefit calculations. Since Third-Way philosophy emphasized the importance of inclusiveness and consensus-building, Blair directed officials in the Treasury to consult with spending departments, cabinet committees, and business groups to fine-tune his neoliberal policy framework. Formalizing these relationships required the establishment of over 300 task forces dedicated to facilitating greater coordination both within and among central government departments.

Again taking his cues from Bill Clinton (who had won the support of both the business community and the middle class by pinning the blame for the 1991–2 economic recession on the failed policies of the Reagan/Bush era), Blair linked the volatile 'boom-bust' cycles of the Thatcher/Major years to their 'ineffective fiscal and monetary strategies'. Thus, in an effort to encourage investment and growth, the Prime Minister's first major economic initiative following his election victory was to grant the Monetary Policy Committee full operational independence in setting short-term interest rates while retaining the government's prerogative to set an ambitious inflation target of 2.5%. Seeking to win the confidence of investors, Chancellor of the Exchequer Gordon Brown would eventually grant policy independence to the Bank of England after consulting with US Federal Reserve Chairman Alan Greenspan. Strongly endorsing Brown's decision, both the Confederation of British Industry and the British Chambers of Commerce was even more delighted when Blair denounced aggressive union wage bargaining practices allegedly 'threatening economic growth'.

New Labour's fiscal strategies were consciously designed to reduce government borrowing while at the same time bolstering opportunities for business and the middle class. Blair's entrepreneurial sympathies lay especially with individuals and companies capable of generating new venture capital, investing in new technologies, and fuelling research and development. Thus, the government's neoliberal reforms succeeded in broadening the tax base while cutting top income and business tax rates in order to provide incentives for investors. To prevent 'excessive borrowing' for social programmes, Blair adopted what he called the 'Golden Rule' – a measure directing the Treasury to keep public debt from exceeding 40% of the GDP. Moreover, he proclaimed that he would not to seek additional spending for health, education, or social security. Asserting that welfare reform could be implemented without increasing public expenditure or raising taxes – except for a one-time 'windfall tax' on privatized utilities – the Prime Minister endorsed a new welfare-to-work programme modelled on Clinton's 'workfare' model. Given Blair's public commitment to 'social justice', his neoliberal social policy agenda came as a shock to many of his working-class supporters. And yet, while still in opposition, both Blair and Brown had already emphasized that the government's guarantee of welfare provisions also required 'accountability' and 'responsibility' from those drawing on these resources.

Overall, then, New Labour social policy focused on reconfiguring three basic services: assistance to the unemployed, assistance to the working poor, and reform of the National Health Service (NHS). Ironically, in pursuing these objectives, Blair was largely inspired by Thatcher's bold, albeit largely unsuccessful, attempts to reform the welfare state by making its administrative functions and procedures more efficient. Accepting Thatcher's argument that 'more money was not the answer', the Prime Minister sought to transform the 'paternalistic' British welfare system into an American-style, neoliberal workfare programme known as the 'New Deal'. But, in direct contrast to FDR's Keynesian-based programme, Blair's New Deal would further liberalize work training schemes by replacing Thatcher's Training and Enterprise Council with an even more neoliberal 'partnership' model. At the same time, however, the Blair government promoted clearly progressive initiatives such as the Working Families Tax Credit to aid the working poor or the adoption of a national minimum wage to assist low-income workers. These seemingly opposed social policy strategies exposed the difficulties of constructing a viable Third Way beyond Left and Right.

Neoliberalism and ethics in foreign policy

Second-wave neoliberal leaders harboured some sympathies for the foreign policy preferences of 'neoliberal institutionalists' who emphasized ethics and humanitarianism as goods in themselves and rejected 'realist' models that saw military and diplomatic policy as mere tools used for the sake of securing and advancing national power. This is not to say that Clinton and Blair jettisoned national interest in favour of some lofty ideal of cosmopolitanism. But for market globalists who believed in the link between the global expansion of commerce and a more peaceful world, moral values like reciprocity and human rights had to play an important role in international relations. Indeed, Clinton and Blair worked closely together in redefining the role of international institutions such as NATO from a Western military alliance created to keep the Soviet bloc in check to a global, multi-purpose organization dedicated to enhancing international security primarily through the protection of human rights and the carrying out of peacekeeping missions.

A clear example of such an approach can be found in the Balkan Wars that began with the 1991 secession of Slovenia

Neoliberal institutionalism

Neoliberal institutionalism is closely associated with the idea of 'institution-building' in order to enhance world trade and global security. It draws its inspiration from two related liberal doctrines: *liberal internationalism* and *economic liberalism*. Liberal internationalism involves using a variety of international policy instruments such as humanitarian aid, diplomacy, and, only when absolutely necessary, military intervention to defend or spread liberal values like democracy and human rights. Two examples would be US President Woodrow Wilson's attempt to establish a League of Nations and the United Nations' promotion of 'collective security' and the rule of law. As we have seen in Chapter 1, economic liberalism is closely connected to the idea of a global free-trade regime built around powerful international economic institutions like the WTO, the IMF, and the World Bank.

from the Socialist Federal Republic of Yugoslavia and ended with the NATO intervention in Serbian and Serb-dominated Kosovo in spring 1999. During the early stages of the Balkan Wars, then presidential candidate Bill Clinton argued that it was up to the European Union to exert proper leadership to bring the conflict to an end by using all diplomatic and non-interventionist means at its disposal. However, when the fighting between Croats and Serbs intensified in Bosnia in 1993–4, Clinton led a drawn-out diplomatic initiative that finally came to fruition in the 1995 Dayton Agreement, effectively ending the war in Bosnia. However, when the continuing conflict in the Albanian-populated area of Kosovo appeared to be immune to similar US-led diplomatic efforts, Clinton and Blair saw no choice but to resort to military intervention by NATO. Justifying the bombing of Serbia as an effort to prevent a widening of 'ethnic cleansing' campaigns undertaken by hard-line Serbian leader Slobodan Milošević, the American President's decision was partially influenced by the public perception that previous acts of ethnic cleansing and genocide in Bosnia and Rwanda (1994) had been enabled by the painfully slow process of negotiations and the related reluctance of the United States and the international community to use military force while these diplomatic efforts were still underway.

And yet, the rationale for the NATO intervention in Kosovo was couched in the liberal language of 'moral imperative' rather than the realist idiom of 'national interest'. In other words, the campaign was justified explicitly on humanitarian grounds: to prevent ethnic cleansing and protect the Kosovar Albanian majority in the Serb-ruled province. In his celebrated speech to the Chicago Economic Club in April 1999 – shortly after the successful conclusion of the NATO campaign against Serbia – Tony Blair proposed a 'doctrine of international community' based on traditional Christian 'just war' teachings that permitted collective acts of violence against implacable aggressors to prevent humanitarian disasters.

The Blair Doctrine

In determining whether there was a moral case for the international community to launch a military strike against a nation, the Blair Doctrine proposed that the following five questions had to be answered in the affirmative. Of course, this was not meant to be an absolute test but rather a basic thematic framework for the issues to be taken into account in decision-making.

1. Are we sure of our case?
2. Have we exhausted all diplomatic options?
3. Are there military operations we can sensibly and prudently undertake?
4. Are we prepared for the long term?
5. Do we have national interests involved?

Conclusion

Anchored in the strategic imperative of growing the economy without falling prey to the divisiveness of old-style partisan politics, second-wave neoliberalism in the 1990s represented an innovative blend of market-oriented thinking and moderate social policies. Seeking to synthesize market-oriented economic growth within an ethical framework of social justice and human rights, both Bill Clinton's market globalism and Tony Blair's Third Way reflected a clear understanding that the age of relatively sheltered national economies had passed and no country could any longer shield its economy from the dynamics of corporate-led globalization.

But critics on the political Left accused second-wave neoliberals of engaging in a largely symbolic rhetoric of 'community' while, in fact, continuing the turbo-capitalist projects of Reaganomics and Thatcherism. Reluctantly acknowledging the economic vibrancy of the Roaring Nineties, these critics nonetheless pointed to extreme levels of inequality in both the global North and South as evidence for the skewed prosperity produced by second-wave neoliberal policies. On the other hand, supporters of market globalism praised its ability to fuel robust economic growth, and supply consumers in the developed world with inexpensive consumer goods from the developing world that also helped raise living standards in those disadvantaged regions. Indeed, it is to the global South that we now must turn to continue our exploration and evaluation of the varieties of neoliberalism.

Chapter 4
Neoliberalism and Asian development

Although the impact of first- and second-wave neoliberalisms on Asian countries in the last quarter century has been considerable, it should be noted that these market-oriented ideas of liberalization, deregulation, and privatization had to contend with a strong tradition of state interventionism and economic centralism. The bonds between the state and the private sector run especially deep in the region – a dynamic that has been especially well documented in East and Southeast Asian countries.

As the World Bank emphasized, 'between the mid-1960s and 1990, eight Asian countries – Japan, the four *Asian Tigers* (Hong Kong, South Korea, Singapore, and Taiwan), and the three newly industrializing economies of Indonesia, Malaysia, and Thailand – enjoyed growth rates double those of the rest of the region, three times those of Latin America and South Asia, and five times those of sub-Saharan Africa'. The 1993 *World Bank Report* characterized such astonishing economic success as the 'Asian miracle' and attributed it to high rates of private investment that complemented 'sound development policies' and 'skilled macroeconomic management'. Although at times contested, this thriving 'Asian Development Model' seemed to underline that close government-business cooperation within a homegrown cultural framework was the best path to rapid economic growth in Asia.

The Asian Development Model

The Asian Development Model rests on cooperative relations among government, business, and labour. Sometimes also referred to as 'corporatism', this model has four basic features:

1. relatively autonomous rule by a political-bureaucratic state elite strong enough to repel interest-group pressures to adopt short-term economic policies over long-term economic growth strategies;

2. public–private sector cooperation resulting in national 'industrial policies' geared toward upgrading the manufacturing industry and increasing exports (these policies are overseen by government planning agencies);

3. public investment in education to develop competitive labour markets;

4. disciplined protection of domestic markets from foreign imports (and domestic control over the capital market).

Directing new flows of capital into high-yielding investments and new technologies, Asian governments intervened in their domestic financial markets by channeling money to selected industrial sectors that sustained high levels of productivity such as heavy industry. But, as we shall see below, the Asian Development Model experienced serious challenges in the 1980s. Many economists credit the region's subsequent turn toward neoliberalism with the high levels of economic growth in the early 1990s, particularly in Southeast Asia. The lifting of financial regulations on foreign

The Asian Financial Crisis

In the 1990s, the governments of Thailand, Indonesia, Malaysia, South Korea, and the Philippines gradually abandoned control over the domestic movement of capital in order to attract foreign direct investment. Intent on creating a stable money environment, they raised domestic interest rates and linked their national currencies to the value of the US dollar. The ensuing irrational euphoria of international investors translated into soaring stock and real-estate markets all over Southeast Asia. However, by 1997, those investors realized that prices had become inflated much beyond their actual value. They panicked and swiftly withdrew a total of $105 billion from these countries, forcing governments in the region to abandon the dollar peg. Unable to halt the ensuing free-fall of their currencies, those governments used up their entire foreign exchange reserves. As a result, economic output fell, unemployment increased, and wages plummeted. Foreign banks and creditors reacted by declining new credit applications and refusing to extend existing loans. By late 1997, the entire region found itself in the throes of a financial crisis that threatened to push the global economy into recession. This disastrous result was only narrowly averted by a combination of international bailout packages and the immediate sale of Southeast Asian commercial assets to foreign corporate investors at rock-bottom prices. Even today, many ordinary citizens in Southeast Asia are still suffering from the devastating social and political consequences of that economic meltdown.

capital also encouraged a flood of speculative foreign investments and extreme financial volatility. In 1997, however, the boom years came to a sudden end with the Asian Financial Crisis whose devastating impact was felt in the region for years.

Let us now examine why and how various Asian governments decided to modify their economic models in a neoliberal direction. As we shall see, political leaders such as Prime Ministers Ryutaro Hashimoto and Junichiro Koizumi of Japan, Chinese Presidents Jiang Zemin and Hu Jintao, and Indian Prime Minister Manmohan Singh have embraced certain aspects of neoliberalism in an effort to enhance the economic performance of their respective countries.

Although they did not run their national economies exclusively according to Anglo-American free-market principles, they nonetheless acknowledged the importance of private-sector-driven economic growth in increasingly globally integrated markets.

Japan: state developmentalism meets neoliberalism

Focusing primarily on the export oriented production of consumer goods, large Japanese industrial groups known as *keiretsu* forged after World War II a close alliance with the country's dominant Liberal Democratic Party (LDP). The Ministry of International Trade and Industry (MITI) emerged as the most powerful government agency, overseeing industrial policy, funding research, and directing investment. Promoting domestic industry by protecting it from foreign competition, MITI managed Japanese trade and industry almost along the lines of a centrally planned economy. By the 1970s, Japan not only had caught up with the West in several key industry sectors such as automobiles and consumer electronics, but had surpassed the productivity of the world's most powerful economies. Japan's financial markets remained under the strict control of the Ministry of Finance (MOF), which managed both interest rates and foreign exchange rates. While the US saw private savings slip dramatically during the 1970s, Japan's savings rate reached an impressive 20%, which comes close to what many economists consider the optimal level for self-sustaining economic growth. A little more than a decade later, however, the Japanese economy showed signs of severe strain. What had happened?

Acting on directives from MITI and MOF, the Japan Development Bank had for decades extended funding via private banks to select types of industries. In picking winners and losers, the state had assumed most of the entrepreneurial risks and allowed the private sector to reap the benefits. But this state-run financing system had insulated private firms from short-term market imperatives and fluctuations, allowing them to engage in long-term economic planning according to rigid industrial policies. Under this arrangement, Japanese companies could afford to take higher risks by investing in innovative products without having to respond to the short-term interests of stockholders who demanded immediate profits on their investments (as was the case with Japan's Western competitors).

Rooted in traditional principles akin to economic nationalism, the system provided a partly privatized welfare-state arrangement for the employees of major Japanese firms. Many managers and workers enjoyed lifetime employment – an arrangement that promoted a strong sense of mutual loyalty while also encouraging managers to engage in long-term strategic thinking. A major drawback of this socially conscious system, however, was that firms could not easily adjust to shifting market conditions. When confronted with dwindling profits and severe capital shortages due to the fledgling dynamics of globalization, Japan's businesses found it extremely difficult to embrace hard-nosed, 'neoliberal' measures such as reducing personal expenditures by 'downsizing' the workforce. But when an inflated real-estate market and seriously overvalued stocks further slowed down the Japanese economy, the pressure on the government to consider such measures grew significantly. Further economic shocks, and President George H. W. Bush's persistent demands to open up protected Japanese markets to more US imports, forced the Japanese government to reassess its conventional economic practices.

A number of reform-minded politicians led by Prime Minister Ryutaro Hashimoto began to experiment with neoliberal

Tokyo's 'Big Bang'

Under the leadership of Prime Minister Hashimoto, Tokyo's financial system underwent in the mid-1990s a neoliberal transformation similar to that of London's 'Big Bang' ten years earlier. In the previous decade, the volume of shares traded on the Tokyo stock exchange had dropped more than 50%, allowing competing financial markets in Hong Kong and Singapore to pick up a huge share of Japan's business. But Hashimoto's reform package included a drastic deregulation clause aimed at removing the legal barriers prohibiting banks from merging with insurance firms or dealing in securities. The 1996 laws also removed regulations governing brokerage commissions and encouraged foreign investment. Like Thatcher, Hashimoto transformed Tokyo's insulated stock exchange into a vibrant global financial centre.

measures, in the process altering traditional corporatist government–business relationships in Japan. Under intense public pressure to react to the deteriorating economic situation, Hashimoto announced in 1996 a comprehensive reform package containing obvious neoliberal measures.

In addition, the Japanese government resorted to monetarist remedies aimed at lowering interest rates to zero. Other neoliberal measures, like the 2001 Quantitative Monetary Easing Policy, sought to increase the country's money supply after the collapse of several banks burdened with large quantities of non-performing loans. While these initiatives did ease the economic situation to some extent, they also contributed to deflation, thus failing to lift consumer confidence.

Succeeding Hashimoto, the energetic Prime Minister Junichiro Koizumi promised to treat the anaemic Japanese economy with a generous dose of *kozo kaikaku* – the neoliberal restructuring of Japan's 'national structure'. In a politically risky manoeuvre, in 2005, Koizumi sought to privatize the Japanese Postal Savings system – the world's largest bank, holding £1.75 trillion in savings. But this was not an easy task, given that the Japanese Postal

Savings was intimately tied to the country's traditional elites, who were reluctant to tinker with such a 'unique national feature'. Accused of capitulating to the Western forces of market globalism, the reform-minded Prime Minister encountered fierce opposition. After an intense battle with some of his own party members, Koizumi was forced to compromise, promising that such a large privatization measure would not be finalized until 2017 – and could even be repealed by any future prime minister! Still, the deflated leader managed to score a few neoliberal victories by

11. Junichiro Koizumi (1932–), Prime Minister of Japan (2001–6)

reforming the state housing corporation and opening up the mortgage business to private non-bank companies.

In the end, however, the achievements of Junichiro Koizumi's *kozo kaikaku* initiative remained rather modest, especially when measured against second-wave neoliberalism in Britain and the United States. Unlike Clinton, Koizumi failed to reduce the massive national budget deficit because the required cuts to expenditures were not approved by key power blocs in his own LDP and the state bureaucracy. Still, the impact of his neoliberal reforms on Japan's economy is evident in its global integration. Moreover, there is no question that the *kozo kaikaku* reforms have introduced new market-based approaches and practices, thus altering Japan's traditional state-managed model.

China: 'neoliberalism with Chinese characteristics'

Market-oriented reforms undertaken by three successive post-Maoist governments in China have been hailed by neoliberal proponents as the drivers of the country's stunning economic success as measured by its average annual GDP growth rate of 9.7% over the last two decades. The transformation of China's economic system was a gradual process, but the spread of Western neoliberal ideas, particularly among urban elites, occurred much more quickly. Today, China is the world's third largest economy, rapidly narrowing the gap with Japan and the United States. Some of the country's premier institutions of higher education such as Beijing's Tsinghua University or Shanghai's Fudan University offer business courses that are virtually identical to those run by first-rate Western universities. Indeed, the writings of neoliberal icons such as Milton Friedman, Frederick Hayek, and James Buchanan have been translated into Chinese and enjoy brisk sales.

China's turn toward neoliberalism began in the late 1970s after 30 years of economic planning and political centralism presided over by Mao Zedong. At the time of his death in 1976, millions of ordinary

Chinese had paid the ultimate price for the Chairman's totalitarian vision. Devastating famines had followed forced industrialization in the 1950s, grandiosely termed the 'Great Leap Forward'. The political persecutions of the 'Great Proletarian Cultural Revolution' in the late 1960s had killed or incarcerated millions. With the regime's crimes of the past still casting a dark shadow in the 1970s, the pragmatic reorientation of China's economy toward market principles would have been impossible without a fundamental ideological revision of orthodox 'Mao Zedong Thought'.

This task fell to the ageing leader Deng Xiaoping, who emerged as the unlikely architect of what political economist David Harvey calls 'neoliberalism with Chinese characteristics'. A tough political survivor who had been stripped of his influential party posts twice during the Cultural Revolution on charges of being a 'capitalist roader', Deng engineered his full rehabilitation after Mao's death with the support of a pragmatic Old Guard that had lost much of its power during the Cultural Revolution. Moving cautiously but resolutely against Maoist hard-liners in his party, Deng spearheaded a nationwide campaign to 'emancipate the mind, unite, and look ahead'. Draped in the disingenuous rhetoric of continuing the Great Leader's communist vision, 'Dengism' represented a genuine search for an alternative model – state-socialism-plus-market, to be evaluated according to the neoliberal criteria of economic efficiency, productivity, and competitiveness. In 1978, the Chinese Communist Party (CCP) endorsed Deng's economic reform package, which abandoned Mao's doctrine of 'continual class struggle' in favour of economic construction and modernization. It also called for the gradual devolution of economic and political power to local and regional bodies without compromising the party's cardinal principle of central decision-making. Finally, it mandated a gradual, state-controlled process of 'opening up' to the West for the expressed purpose of 'learning advanced management and new technologies from foreign countries'. In spite of its remarkable turn toward the market, however, Dengism made abundantly clear that the state remained

12. **Chinese Leader Deng Xiaoping (1904–97)**

the sole institution endowed with the crucial power of legalizing
new forms of economic enterprise; setting prices and wages;
supervising of imports and foreign direct investment; and

permitting domestic firms to export their goods to various international destinations.

Economic restructuring under Deng is most notably associated with the privatization of State-Owned Enterprises (SOEs). For three decades, these industrial collectives had guaranteed secure employment and welfare provisions to their mostly urban workers. The agrarian sector of the planned economy was organized around rather inefficient communal farming. Forced to endure strict segregation practices that limited their movements, rural workers received lower welfare benefits than urban workers. As Deng's market reforms picked up steam in the 1980s, SOEs began employing short-term contract workers – especially from rural areas – without having to provide them with the same generous social benefits guaranteed to permanent workers. Firm directors were offered greater operational discretion to run their SOEs more efficiently and were even allowed to keep some surplus goods produced above their state-mandated quotas. Sold in the 'open market', the prices of these products were considerably higher than the official prices set by the state. Thus, profits accruing to budding manager-entrepreneurs were often substantial. These diverging pricing practices, however, proved to be unsustainable as managers sought to increase their share of goods at the expense of the state quotas. The productivity of SOEs declined significantly, forcing state-owned banks to subsidize these failing enterprises, which quickly depleted China's finances. Responding to these problems in 1993, the CCP leadership decided to allow the transformation of a small number of handpicked SOEs into shareholding companies. Shortly after, further privatization reforms turned additional state enterprises into joint stock corporations. Indeed, the privatization of SOEs would continue at a dramatic rate throughout the next two decades.

The next major step in Beijing's privatization scheme was the CCP's decision to open up some SOEs to foreign ownership. The ensuing flood of foreign direct investment greatly contributed to the emergence of China as an industrial superpower, especially as the world's hub of labour-intensive manufacturing. 'Special Enterprise Zones' (SEZs) created by the government mostly along four major Chinese coastal cities further facilitated the export-based production of consumer goods while serving as research and development centres where young Chinese business leaders

Tsingtao Brewery goes neoliberal

Tsingtao Brewery goes back almost a century. Originally the brainchild of German entrepreneurs in 1903, the company was seized in 1949 by Qingdao's local government and run according to command-style communist planning imperatives. High production costs, low outputs, and a burgeoning bureaucracy resulted in limited sales and low profits on exports. In 1993, Tsingtao was reorganized into a joint-stock company. Within a few years, both productivity and output rose dramatically. The company attracted prominent domestic and foreign investors, including leading Chinese banks and the Anheuser-Busch corporation. Today, over half of Tsingtao Brewery shares are in private hands.

absorbed new technologies and managerial practices. SEZs attracted foreign capital by offering incentives, including tax breaks and secured-risk arrangements according to which profits were paid to foreign firms in advance. Moreover, the Chinese government signed off on massive investments in new infrastructure.

Seeking to stabilize its currency, the Chinese government tacitly pegged the Yuan to the American dollar in 1995. But the state retained strong control over capital flows and signalled its unwillingness to make the Yuan fully convertible. Western political economists tend to argue that China has consistently engaged in exchange rate manipulations in order to increase the competitiveness of its global exports. Bemoaning their country's widening trade deficit with China – $233 billion in 2007 – US

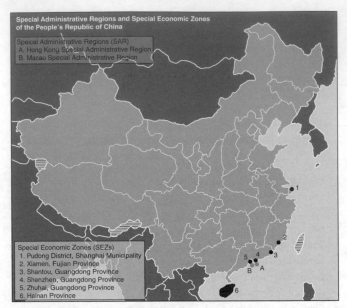

Special Administrative Regions and Special Economic Zones of the People's Republic of China

Speical Administrative Regions (SAR)
A. Hong Kong Special Administrative Region
B. Macau Special Administrative Region

Special Economic Zones (SEZs)
1. Pudong District, Shanghai Municipality
2. Xiamen, Fujian Province
3. Shantou, Guangdong Province
4. Shenzhen, Guangdong Province
5. Zhuhai, Guangdong Province
6. Hainan Province

Map 1. China's Special Enterprise Zones

Source: http://en.wikipedia.org/wiki/File:PR_China-SAR_%26_SEZ-English.png

Treasury officials have estimated that the Yuan could be undervalued by as much as 40%.

The gradual extension of neoliberal reforms in China over the last two decades did not always proceed smoothly. Already the 1989 Tiananmen Square massacre of hundreds of pro-democracy protestors had brought to the fore the fundamental contradiction at the heart of Chinese society: how can the regime extend market reforms without jeopardizing its hold on political power? Fearful that future popular uprisings might succeed in undermining the authority of the state – as they had done in the Soviet Union and Eastern Europe – the government responded to Tiananmen with severe political repression. Although it managed to avoid a Soviet-style collapse of the system, the CCP failed to remove the

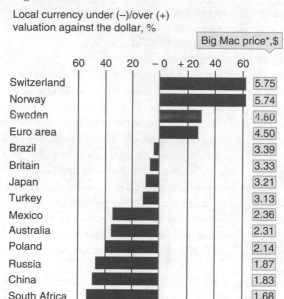

Big Mac Index

Local currency under (−)/over (+)
valuation against the dollar, %

Big Mac price*,$

	60	40	20	− 0 +	20	40	60	
Switzerland								5.75
Norway								5.74
Sweden								4.60
Euro area								4.50
Brazil								3.39
Britain								3.33
Japan								3.21
Turkey								3.13
Mexico								2.36
Australia								2.31
Poland								2.14
Russia								1.87
China								1.83
South Africa								1.68

* At market exchange rate (January 19th)
† Weighted average of member countries

E. The Big Mac Index and the undervalued Yuan
The *Economist*'s Big Mac Index provides a basic illustration of the
Purchasing Price Parity Index (PPP), which suggests that prices for
products should be comparable across nations. In this case, the prices
of Big Mac meals are regularly compared as an estimate to determine
whether the currency of a given country is valued appropriately. After
being converted into US dollars, if the price of a Big Mac meal is higher
than $3.54 (a baseline of zero in this particular index) the currency is
considered to be undervalued. Since a Big Mac meal in China is sold for
a mere $1.83, it shows that the Yuan is undervalued by over 40 percent.

Source: Extra value meal: 26 January, 2009, from economist.com, 'Britain and Japan inch
closer to the benchmark'.

underlying contradiction between its marketization drive and its
deeply ingrained authoritarian tendencies. By the time of Deng
Xiaoping's death in 1997, the party had finally settled on a less
repressive compromise: to buy popular legitimacy by means of

global economic integration that would raise the living standards of most Chinese people. But it remains to be seen if this inherently unstable 'neoliberalism with Chinese characteristics' can continue to coexist with a centralized one-party state.

Deng's successor, President Jiang Zemin, further shifted the public discourse from the old socialist values of egalitarianism and redistribution to the new neoliberal objectives of economic growth and profit maximization. At the same time, however, his efforts stopped considerably short of the free-market ideal envisioned by the Washington Consensus. In spite of its membership in the WTO and its support of young business entrepreneurs and managers, China's economic transition remains firmly in the hands of powerful political factions that are increasingly divided into the bureaucratic-nationalistic centralists in Beijing and more entrepreneurial-globalist locals in Shanghai, Guangzhou, Chongqing, and other major urban centres.

Since assuming power in 2003, President Hu Jingtao has pressed forward with neoliberal reforms in such critical areas as science and technology, intellectual property rights, and trade policy. At the same time, however, his government has remained committed to a state-managed transition to a market system. For example, the CCP continues to control the prices and supply of water and power. It also subsidizes the inefficient energy sector, which feeds the country's gigantic manufacturing base. Without such government subsidies, Chinese industry would be hard pressed to compete globally. Indeed, one of its most tenacious competitors is India, which, like China, transformed its socialistic, mixed economy along neoliberal lines.

India: mixed economy meets market globalism

Since 2003, India has recorded an impressive average GDP growth rate of 8.8% per year. This economic achievement, however, came hand-in-hand with widening disparities of income and wellbeing in the wake of an unprecedented set of neoliberal reforms launched in the 1990s. Manmohan Singh, India's former Finance Minister and current Prime Minister, has been the architect of the biggest economic growth his country has ever seen. There is little doubt that India's success has been driven largely by a thriving computer industry and high-tech services, both of which comprise more than 50% of the country's total productive output. Indeed, productivity and innovation have also surged in manufacturing. For example, India's automobile giant, Tata Motors, has made international headlines with its fuel-efficient, globally marketed 'Nano' model – a small 'people's car' that went on sale domestically in early 2009 for less than $3,000. But this 'Indian miracle' must be understood within the context of the country's economic development, which occurred in three historical stages: the socialist era (1947–84); the period of what economist Arvind Panagariya has called 'liberalization by stealth' (1984–91); and the current stage of what economist Jagdish Bhagwati has termed 'reform by storm' (1991 to the present).

In the first period, India's economic course was plotted by two dynamic leaders – Jawaharlal Nehru and his daughter Indira Gandhi. His country's first Prime Minister following independence from British colonial rule in 1947, Nehru chose a democratic-socialist middle way between the capitalist West and the communist Soviet bloc by rejecting both Western 'liberal' economic ideas such as free trade and entrepreneurial individualism and Marxist-Leninist forms of authoritarian collectivism. Promising to safeguard India's national sovereignty, the charismatic Prime Minister championed a 'mixed-economy' approach, which placed the principal means of production into the hands of the state with the expressed goal of ensuring an equitable distribution of the nation's productive output. Impressed by the ideas of Fabian democratic socialism with which he had become acquainted during his university years at Cambridge, Nehru envisioned an India where economic state planning and democracy were seamlessly reconciled. This vision inspired a series of government-led Five-Year Plans based on a command-and-control model that focused on developing heavy industry and manufacturing. The private sector was to be subordinated to the state and business licences were only issued for purposes that met the government's planning objectives. Relying on hundreds of state-controlled factories, Nehru's economic nationalism was bought at the price of economic productivity and growth. Grossly inefficient and largely unresponsive to the people's material needs, only nine of these state-run firms turned a profit. Moreover, the agricultural sector was largely neglected, although 80% of the population lived and worked in rural areas.

When Indira Gandhi came to power in 1966, she actually expanded her father's economic model by nationalizing the largest banks and insurance companies as well as some energy industries. Deeply suspicious of free-market philosophies, she went on to nationalize a number of Indian subsidiaries of powerful multinational corporations such as Coca-Cola, in the process thwarting foreign direct investment for many years to come. Nationalization of the banking sector, however, had the problematic effect of managers issuing loans on the basis of political patronage rather than according to sound financial considerations. As a result, the number of non-performing loans increased dramatically, putting India's entire economy in peril.

Succeeding his mother after her assassination in 1984, Prime Minister Rajiv Gandhi cautiously opened the door to a series of mild neoliberal reforms that eased government restrictions on some industries by removing licensing requirements and liberalizing some export regulations. Through tax cuts and the reduction of tariffs on capital goods, Gandhi managed to enhance the convertibility of the rupee, which, in turn, led to a significant increase in trade. Though limited in both their approach and scope, the Prime Minister's neoliberal reforms delivered an unprecedented, albeit short-lived, period of economic growth. But factional struggles within the governing Congress Party over Rajiv Gandhi's neoliberal reform initiatives, accompanied by a major corruption scandal implicating the Prime Minister himself, brought his efforts to a grinding halt.

And yet, the success of Rajiv Gandhi's market reforms, no matter how limited, marked the end of an era. Once the neoliberal genie had escaped the bottle, it proved to be difficult to get it back in. In fact, unleashing 'neoliberal reform by storm' appeared to be a real option in a country sliding into a full-blown fiscal crisis stemming from a massive problem that had been mounting over the course of the decade. In 1991, India's national debt approached 50% of the GDP. Servicing these loans devoured valuable foreign reserves that had already been reduced to dangerously low levels. To avoid a major default, the Indian government turned to the IMF for a massive $1.8 billion bailout package. In the midst of this crisis, Narashima Rao succeeded the assassinated Rajiv Gandhi. The reform-minded Prime Minister lost no time in appointing the Oxford-trained economist Manmohan Singh Finance Minister, empowering him to launch a sweeping set of neoliberal reforms that would dramatically alter the country's economic landscape. Viewing the crisis as an historic opportunity to 'build a new India', Singh argued that it was essential to terminate 'outmoded' commitments to Nehru's economic nationalism. Spouting with gusto French novelist Victor Hugo's line that 'no power on earth can stop an idea whose time has come', the new Finance Minister promised to realize his neoliberal vision by building on his country's vast and cheap labour markets, its growing number of educated, but unemployed, professionals, and its considerable natural resources.

Neoliberal reforms enacted in India since 1991

- Rescinding state licence requirements for most industries.
- Cutting the tariff rate on imports.
- Exchange rate liberalization, increasing the convertibility of the rupee.
- Courting foreign direct investment by easing restrictions.

- Removing limits on large corporations to compete in new economic sectors.
- Privatization of state-owned industries.
- Lowering the cash reserve requirements.

Convinced by the claims of Western market globalists and determined to put India on the track to becoming a global economic power, Singh believed that the adoption of a fiscal austerity package and strict monetary policies – in conjunction with sizeable structural adjustment programmes from the IMF – would unleash India's entrepreneurial potential. In the first half of the 1990s, he cut taxes and simplified the national tax system; slashed tariffs on imports; dispensed with the state's licensing requirements for most industries; corrected India's exchange rate irregularities; privatized key state-run industries; and encouraged foreign direct investment. After he became Prime Minister in May 2004, Singh further expanded and accelerated his neoliberal reforms. Proclaiming that the biggest obstacle to India's success in the global economy was the poor condition of its roads, ports, and energy plants, Singh pressed for the formation of public–private

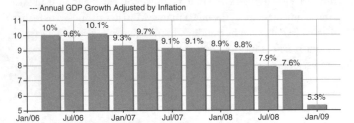

F. India's GDP growth rate, 2006–9

In 2007–08 India's total domestic productive output was three trillion dollars (measured in PPP terms) which spurred a 9.1 percent growth rate making it second only to China as the fastest-expanding economy. However, the figure above suggests that the global recession is impacting the growth.

Source: http://www.tradingeconomics.com/Economics/GDP-Growth.aspx?Symbol=INR.

13. Manmohan Singh (1932–), Prime Minister of India (2004–)

partnerships to overhaul the country's infrastructure and supply its businesses and villages with cheap and reliable electricity.

To meet his ambitious energy and infrastructure targets, the Prime Minister committed his country to the development of nuclear power. Acknowledging that India could not develop such capacities on its own, Singh sought assistance from the global community. Reversing Nehru's critical stance toward the United States, Singh accepted George W. Bush's invitation to enter into a genuine economic and political partnership. Recognizing the subcontinent's strategic importance as a potential ally against rising China and global terrorism, the American President became a leading advocate for supplying India with cutting-edge nuclear technology. After a long and arduous struggle with domestic legislators who refused to grant India special exception to the Non-Nuclear Proliferation Agreement, Bush secured Congressional approval for the US–India Civil Nuclear Deal, which was signed into law in 2008 as the United States–India Nuclear Cooperation Approval and Non-Proliferation Enhancement Act. Its passage was especially gratifying for Manmohan Singh, who had spearheaded a similarly difficult political campaign for ratification of the treaty in his own country.

The positive outcomes of Prime Minister Singh's comprehensive neoliberal reforms are obvious: massive economic growth, exchange rate stability, and, until recently, substantial increases in foreign direct investment. On the downside, however, neoliberal reforms have increased the gap between the rich and the poor. The privatization of housing has put home ownership out of reach for the majority of ordinary Indians. Moreover, economic growth has meant an increase in demand for oil, whose rising price has once again put pressure on India's foreign reserves. Indeed, the budget deficit has risen to 10% of the GDP. Finally, Singh's embrace of market globalism has exposed the country to the devastating impact of the current global financial crisis.

Conclusion

Whether economic change in Asia was driven by imperatives forced upon countries by the dynamics of globalization or was deliberately adopted by these market-oriented leaders to suit their own political objectives, there has been a remarkable shift toward neoliberalism in the region in the last two decades. This ongoing transformation has not been a uniform process; different nations have found unique ways of partaking in an increasingly global marketplace. Distinct neoliberal adaptations evolved within highly differentiated political-economic systems, as illustrated in the three cases discussed in this chapter. Thus, a genuine comparison of its various manifestations in Asia shatters the myth that neoliberalism necessarily comes only in an Anglo-American form. Let us now turn to Latin America and Africa to complete our journey around the world.

Chapter 5
Neoliberalism in Latin America and Africa

The Washington Consensus exercised enormous influence in shaping neoliberal policies in Latin America and Africa. As we noted in Chapter 1, the IMF and World Bank began in the early 1980s linking loan guarantees for heavily indebted developing countries to 'structural adjustment programmes' (SAPs), which mandated that loan-receiving governments restructure their economies according to neoliberal principles. These included putting more emphasis on production for export rather than on meeting the needs of national and local markets; severe spending cuts – especially for social programmes; sweeping privatization measures; reduced regulation on the activities of transnational corporations; and, in a number of cases, significant currency devaluations. Moreover, these international lenders made sure that a large portion of their loans were earmarked for servicing external debts these countries had accumulated as a result of several factors: deep-seated patterns of social domination left behind by colonialism; misguided development strategies often devised by First World aid agencies; the dramatic oil price hikes of the 1970s; the rise of global interest rates in the early 1980s; waning global demand for Third World products; decreasing importance of domestic markets; ill-considered and wasteful mega-construction projects; and widespread corruption among domestic governing elites.

Let us begin by examining the spread of the neoliberal model to Latin America in the 1980s and 1990s by focusing on three countries: Chile, Argentina, and Mexico. In the former two cases, the imposition of the Washington Consensus was preceded by sustained academic attacks on Latin American economic practices. Dominating the region in the 1950s and 1960s, such 'developmentalism' was largely derived from principles of economic nationalism based on the successful path of development taken by most West European and North American countries in the late 19th and early 20th centuries. Developmentalist intellectuals like the Argentine economist Raul Prebisch suggested that economic progress in the region depended on internal industrialization protected by high tariffs and limited trade rather than the export of natural resources to a global market whose prices were controlled by large European and North American corporations. Developmentalist politicians translated these theories into economic policy by supporting the nationalization of key industries such as mining and transportation. As long as private enterprises supported state-directed economic development projects, they were offered public subsidies to build factories and hire workers. The state also put into place stringent price controls for food and other basic products. The successful execution of these economic objectives required a highly centralized and interventionist government committed to national autonomy and some basic welfare provisions such as social services and public education.

Chile and Argentina

As early as the 1950s, members of the Chicago School of Economics were eager to extend their public criticism of the Keynesian macroeconomic practices of Western democracies to Latin American countries. Strongly opposed to their developmentalist model, Milton Friedman and his colleague Arnold Harberger enlisted the help of the University of Chicago, the US State Department, several large American corporations, and the Ford

Foundation to establish neoliberal academic programmes in South America. One of these, the so-called 'Chile Project', trained hundreds of Chilean economics students – henceforth known in the region as 'the Chicago Boys' – both at the University of Chicago and Santiago's Catholic University according to free-market principles. During the 1960s, such programmes were significantly expanded across the region and students of these gradually rose to prominent academic and government positions in countries such as Argentina, Uruguay, and Brazil.

On 11 September 1973, General Augusto Pinochet staged a CIA-supported coup that overthrew Chile's democratically elected President Salvador Allende, a strong supporter of the developmentalist school. Immediately after the military's seizure of power, several homegrown 'Chicago Boys' presented Chile's new strongman with a 500-page economic blueprint for the country's economy. Known as 'The Brick', this document called for extensive and immediate deregulation and privatization measures as well as deep cuts to social spending, the reduction of tariffs, and the lifting of price controls – ostensibly for the purpose of fighting Chile's runaway inflation. Accepting large parts of this programme, Pinochet hastily proceeded to impose these neoliberal policies at break-neck speed while clamping down on his political opponents. While conceding that the general's brutal methods of political repression hardly dovetailed with their libertarian ideals, Friedman and Hayek nonetheless argued that such neoliberal shock treatments ought to be given a 'fair chance', predicting that their swift application would return Chile to democracy, freedom, and unprecedented levels of prosperity.

But Pinochet would hold extensive dictatorial powers for the next two decades, which remained marred by frequent disappearances of political dissidents, torture, and other systemic violations of human rights. During his authoritarian rule, Chile's economy stabilized in terms of inflation and GDP growth rate, but the middle and lower classes lost ground as economic inequality increased dramatically. The country's richest 10% benefited the most from the neoliberal reforms as their incomes almost doubled during the Pinochet years. To this day, Chile has remained one of world's 15 most unequal nations. The mixed economic results of the 'neoliberal revolution' that swept the country from the 1970s to the 1990s continue to generate heated discussions among proponents and detractors of the Chicago School over the virtues of externally imposed free-market reforms.

Argentina faced a similar situation in 1976 when a military junta consisting of three generals seized power from the democratically

Columbia	53.8 (2005)
Chile	54.9 (2003)
Guatemala	55.1 (2007)
Panama	56.1 (2003)
Bosnia and Herzegovina	56.2 (2007)
Brazil	56.7 (2005)
Paraguay	56.8 (2008)
Haiti	59.2 (2001)
Bolivia	59.2 (2006)
Central African Republic	61.3 (1993)
Sierra Leone	62.9 (1989)
Botswana	63 (1993)
Lesotho	63.2 (1995)
South Africa	65 (2005)
Namibia	70.7 (2003)

G. The 15 most unequal nations in the world
The Gini Coefficient is a statistical method of income and wealth distribution within a country. A comparatively higher score indicates that wealth and income is more unequally distributed whereas a lower score indicates that they are more evenly distributed.

Source: CIA Factbook 2007 [online] at <https://www.cia gov/library/publications/the world-factbook/fields/2172.html>

elected government of President Isabel Perón, the widow of Juan Domingo Perón, founder of the national-populist 'Perónist' party and once the country's most dominant political figure. Maintaining close contacts to homegrown 'Chicago Boys', the ruling generals initiated several neoliberal reforms but refused to go as far as to privatize some key industries as Pinochet had done. With regard to political repression, however, they closely followed the Chilean strongmen's strategy of disappearing and torturing thousands of dissidents they labelled indiscriminately as 'subversives'. As the award-winning economic journalist and writer Naomi Klein has suggested, the Argentine junta's alleged turn toward the 'free market' during its seven-year dictatorial rule actually resembled more closely the model of Fascist corporatism based on the forced collusion of government, business, and trade unions.

After the collapse of the military dictatorship following the generals' disastrous 1982 Falklands campaign against the United Kingdom, the newly elected President Raul Alfonsin found his country teetering on the verge of economic collapse. Saddled with a huge national debt accumulated by the previous regime and threatened by runaway inflation, Alfonsin faced massive food riots on the streets of Buenos Aires and other larger cities. Moreover, he was pressured by the very foreign creditors who had provided the military leadership with massive loans to repay them as soon as possible. The President responded by signing off on modest deregulation measures aimed at promoting trade and tightening the money supply to combat hyperinflation. Regarded as too mild by neoliberal investors and creditors, these reforms did little to restore the country's economic health. Forced to resign in the throes of the deepening recession, Alfonsin surrendered power to the Perónist party, at the time led by the flamboyant Carlos Saul Menem. Sworn in as Argentina's 48th President on 8 July 1989, the former provincial governor promised the electorate that he would never allow the military nor foreign creditors to control the fate of their country.

Thus, most Argentines were shocked when their nationalist-populist President with strong trade union ties refused to revive Latin American developmentalism and instead gave in to the IMF's structural adjustment demands to 'globalize' the country's economy by enacting sweeping neoliberal reforms. Menem proceeded to privatize most publicly owned industries, including the national oil company, the post office, and public utilities like telephone, electricity, and water. Further privatization reforms were instituted in the welfare sector diminishing social security programmes. The Menem administration also made severe cuts to public spending and liberalized capital controls, thus encouraging a flood of mostly speculative foreign investment.

Determined to stay his neoliberal course despite considerable resistance even within his own party, the President curtailed the power of Perónist national-populists by appointing several neoliberal 'Chicago Boys' to important government posts. The most prominent of these appointments, Finance Minister Domingo Cavallo, was entrusted with stabilizing the country's monetary system according to the 1991 Convertibility Law. This controversial act mandated that the country's new currency – the Argentine peso – was to be pegged to the American dollar. This was accomplished by means of a currency board which oversaw the massive acquisition of reserve assets in the form of US bonds. In essence, Argentina's 'dollarized' currency regime ensured that people's pesos could be exchanged at any time and at any bank for US currency – at a fixed rate. Claiming to have exorcized the

Currency boards

Used by Argentina until 2002, a currency board oversees the monetary system of a country whose currency is believed to be unstable and is thus pegged to a more stable and widely used currency such as the US dollar, the British pound, or the euro. The basic demands and tasks of currency boards include:

- The subordinate country must acquire sufficient foreign reserves to ensure that all holders of its own currency can convert them into the reserve currency (e.g., the US dollar) at any time.

- The subordinate currency must be fully convertible against the reserve currency.

- The subordinate country's treasury/central bank abdicates its monetary discretion to print money, although it retains its ability to borrow.

- A currency board does not lend money to commercial banks or manipulate interest rates to increase or decrease the money supply (as a reserve bank does).

demon of hyperinflation for good, Cavallo boasted to have performed the 'Menem Miracle'. In his view, the President's adoption of the IMF-imposed 'shock therapy' would usher in an unprecedented period of prosperity in Argentine history.

For the next few years, the Finance Minister's prediction seemed to be on the mark as Argentina enjoyed low unemployment rates, monetary stability, and strong foreign investment. Productivity soared and exports reached new heights. For most of the 1990s, the economy grew at a strong annual rate of 6%, even managing to overcome a relatively mild and temporary recession in the wake of the 1995 Mexican peso crisis.

But there was also a serious downside to the high and stable value of the dollar-pegged peso: it had become quite expensive to produce goods inside the country, thus opening up the domestic market to a flood of cheap imports that undermined local industries and wiped out tens of thousands of jobs. Indeed, Argentina's IMF-mediated global integration had made its economy more susceptible to external shocks such as the

1997–8 Asian Crisis, the 1998 crash of the Russian economy, and the currency crisis afflicting Brazil in 1999. As a result of the deteriorating world economy, Argentina's access to capital markets dried up. Previously celebrated by IMF and World Bank officials as a 'role model' for developing countries, the proud South American nation was now on the verge of economic collapse.

In January 2002, after months of violent street protests in its major cities, Argentina formally defaulted on its massive public debt of $141 billion. In order to prevent a complete social breakdown, Eduardo Duhalde, the country's fifth president in only two weeks, limited customers' access to their savings deposits and decoupled the peso from the dollar. Within hours, the currency lost a third of its value, robbing ordinary people of the fruits of their labour. 'Argentina is broke, sunk,' the President admitted, 'and the neoliberal model has swept everything away with it'. Economic progress since these dark days has been mixed in Argentina. On the bright side, the country's GDP has grown substantially at a rate of nearly 9% per year, thanks to successful debt restructuring and a reduced debt burden, excellent international financial conditions, and expansionary monetary and fiscal policies. On the other hand, however, inflation reached double-digit levels in 2006. President Nestor Kirchner, a self-styled 'centrist-Perónist', responded to this threat by implementing price and tax agreements with businesses. But his multi-year price freezes on electricity and natural gas rates for residential users only stoked consumption and kept private investment away, leading to restrictions on industrial use and blackouts in 2007.

There is no doubt that Nestor Kirchner and his successor, his wife Cristina, have turned Argentina's economy away from neoliberalism toward a rather moderate variant of developmentalism. For example, Cristina Kirchner announced in 2008 her government's plan to nationalize $30 billion in private

The Group of Twenty

The 'Group of Twenty Finance Ministers and Central Bank Governors' (G-20) is a group of important economic leaders from 19 of the world's largest national economies plus the European Union. Promoting discussion among these leaders, the G-20 seeks to address and shape policy issues pertaining to the promotion of international financial stability. In the wake of the global financial crisis, the G-20 has also met at heads-of-government level, most recently in London on 2 April 2009. Collectively, G-20 economies encompass over 60% of the world population as well as comprising 85% of the global GDP and 80% of world trade.

pension funds to protect retirees from falling stock and bond prices. A vociferous critic of the Washington Consensus, the President has nonetheless been forced to deal with the domestic fallout of the global economic crisis within the international framework of the Group of Twenty.

Mexico

The conditions under which neoliberalism came to Mexico in the early 1980s were similar to those existing in Argentina. In both cases, market-oriented reforms were preceded by the re-evaluation of developmentalist industrialization strategies involving the erection of extensive trade barriers to protect domestic industries from foreign competition. Characterized by strong government intervention through the development and management of state-owned enterprises, the Mexican version of developmentalism achieved social reforms and class compromise at the price of high inflation and slow economic growth. Like South American countries such as Argentina and Brazil, Mexico compensated for its annual fiscal shortfalls during much of the 1970s and early 1980s by borrowing heavily from foreign commercial banks. In

August 1982, Mexico's Finance Minister, Jesus Silva-Herzog, declared that his country would no longer be able to service its national debt. Mexico's default triggered the 1982 Latin American Debt Crisis, during which most private foreign lenders either reduced or halted new loans to the region. Relying on massive IMF bailouts to avoid a social catastrophe, Mexican governments in the late 1980s and 1990s were forced to accept the SAPs that were attached to the much-needed capital infusion.

The neoliberal transformation of Mexico occurred in two major stages under two rather different leaders: Presidents Carlos Salinas de Gatari (1988–94) and Ernesto Zedillo Ponce de León (1994–2000). Salinas's fundamental market reform was accompanied by authoritarian political measures, though less severe than those imposed by Pinochet in Chile. The apex of Salinas's neoliberal reform effort was undoubtedly his country's regional economic integration through the North American Free Trade Agreement (NAFTA). To implement the trade agreement along with the SAPs prescribed by the Washington Consensus, the Salinas administration worked closely with an elite group of US-trained neoliberal economists – Mexico's version of the 'Chicago Boys'. Assembling a powerful market-oriented alliance of economists, policy experts, and business leaders representing the country's largest corporations, the President hoped to attract sizeable foreign direct investments, which he believed to be essential to securing Mexico's long-term, export-oriented economic future.

However, on 1 January 1994 – the day NAFTA came into effect – Mexico's ruling elite unexpectedly found its economic neoliberalism challenged by a popular uprising in the southern state of Chiapas. A left-leaning band of 'national liberation' fighters calling themselves 'Zapatistas', after the agrarian Mexican revolutionary Emiliano Zapata, clashed with government troops in their ultimately unsuccessful attempt to spark a national revolution. They did manage, however, to draw the world's attention to the impact of neoliberal policies on the poor and indigenous populations in the global South. The Chiapas uprising also resulted in a series of nationwide protests aimed at toppling Salinas's government and weakening the power of the Institutional Revolutionary Party (PRI) that had been entrenched for more than six decades. Anti-corruption protesters soon joined this coalition of dissident groups. Political instability and economic uncertainty grew in Mexico with the kidnappings of well-known businessmen and the assassination of the leading PRI presidential candidate, Luis Donaldo Colosio, on 23 March 1994.

Frightened by the deteriorating political situation, investors began withdrawing funds at an alarming rate, thus igniting an economic crisis. Assuming office in these trying times, Salinas's successor, Ernesto Zedillo, attempted to link the newly liberalized economy to a broader democratic political agenda more inclusive of various interest groups. One of the first decisions that the new president had to make was to cut the peso-dollar peg, causing the currency's value to drop by more than 50% in only a few days. In a desperate effort to cement the government's relationship with business and restore investor confidence, Zedillo accepted an IMF bailout package worth nearly $40 billion in exchange for implementing a severe austerity plan that included cutting public spending and raising interest rates. The implementation of these neoliberal measures brought short-term relief to the Mexican economy at the expense of growing social inequality.

Demonstrating his government's commitment to a more open approach to governance, Zedillo initiated discussions with the Zapatistas and eventually came to an agreement introducing changes to the country's Constitution that extended political representation in the nation's legislature to indigenous Mexicans. Promising greater political transparency, Zedillo appointed members of the opposition to key government posts and installed relatively independent judges who, at times, ruled against the government. Finally, the President further engaged in a series of discussions with regional and local politicians in which he

14. Ernesto Zedillo Ponce de León (1951–), President of Mexico (1994–2000)

signalled his willingness to devolve some of his government's central authority. This new trend of combining neoliberal economic reforms with greater political openness continued under the successive presidencies of Vincente Fox Quesada (whose election ended over seven decades of PRI rule) and Felipe Calderón. Although the latter is especially close to free-market circles in the US, the tight results of the 2006 election in Mexico which almost resulted in the victory of anti-NAFTA candidate, Lopez Obrador, suggests the electorate's growing disenchantment with neoliberalism. Indeed, the weak popular mandate for Calderón's neoliberal programme has been further lessened by the current global economic crisis.

Ghana

Having surveyed the impact of the Washington Consensus on Latin America, we should not be surprised to encounter the same overall patterns in Africa as well. Government-led, nationalist developmentalism in the 1950s and 1960s contained an ambitious economic and social agenda beyond the financial capacity of most sub-Saharan African countries. During the next decade, these states turned to both international commercial banks awash in Arab petrodollars and public lenders, in the process managing to triple their debt to $235 billion by the time the Third World Debt Crisis hit in 1982. The stringent SAPs devised by the IMF and World Bank in response to this calamity forced 29 of these countries to adopt the neoliberal model before the decade was over. During the Roaring Nineties, the familiar dynamics of deregulation, liberalization, and privatization measures enforced export-oriented production (especially of monoculture crops and natural resources) at the expense of domestic food production, thus exposing many African countries to famine, epidemics, and ensuing political instability. Thus, despite Africa's adoption of free-market imperatives constructed in the global North, the continent's commodities trade fell from 7% of the world's trade in the mid-1970s to less than 0.5% in the 1990s. Instead of economic recovery and repayment of all external debts, the past quarter century of neoliberalism has seen the lowest rates of economic growth ever recorded in Africa, along with rapidly rising disparities in wealth and wellbeing.

In the dominant discourse of market globalism, Africa's position in the global economy is often described in terms of exclusion and marginalization. Mainstream accounts offered by the World Bank and other international institutions characterize the economic and political development of the entire continent as 'weak', 'dysfunctional', 'poor', 'violent', 'plagued by diseases like AIDS and malaria', 'disintegrating into failed states', and so on. It would hardly be an exaggeration to argue that Africa has almost been written out of the neoliberal globalization story for its alleged 'failure to attract private investment' because of 'bad government', 'corruption', 'lawlessness', and 'endemic civil strife'. But what is left out of this narrative is just as important as what is being emphasized. As we shall see in the case of Ghana, a number of African states have been able to attract substantial external capital, especially for their mineral-extracting industries. According to a report issued by the United Nations Commission on Trade and Development, direct foreign investment in Africa had jumped from 2 billion in 1986 to 15 billion in 2003. While this amount is still rather small measured by world standards, it provides nonetheless hard evidence for challenging the stereotype of an invisible 'global' Africa. Indeed, it appears that the dominant story of an economically and politically irredeemable 'dark continent' skilfully draws on deep-seated colonial images that actually facilitate the extraction of profits by powerful transnational corporations and colluding domestic power elites.

Our brief examination of Ghana will allow us to exemplify these larger socioeconomic changes that have shaped sub-Saharan African nations in the last decades. Let us start by remembering that the social fabric of post-independence Ghana was decisively shaped by President Kwame Nkrumah and his populist Convention People's Party. A champion of economic nationalism and developmentalism, Nkrumah managed to mobilize disenfranchised groups such as labourers and women behind his social vision for a 'new Ghana'. Highly suspicious of Western capitalism, he chose a protectionist path toward industrialization by shielding his country's infant industries from foreign competition. But his strong support of major infrastructure projects such as the Akosombo hydroelectric dam forced him to shift scarce financial resources from the agricultural to the industrial sector. Wedded to a rather authoritarian political style that did not sit well with either traditional rural elites or capitalist modernizers, Nkrumah was overthrown in a 1966 military coup. Two years later, the government led by Kofi Busia flirted with some mild market reforms supporting capital accumulation and market-pricing mechanisms on certain goods. Ghana's economy, however, took a turn for the worse in the 1970s as the price of cocoa – the country's leading agricultural export – plummeted.

In 1979, a military clique led by Air Force Lieutenant Jerry Rawlings staged a successful coup, but his Armed Service Revolutionary Council soon turned over the reins of power to a civilian government headed by Hilla Limann, leader of the People's National Party. In 1981, Rawlings staged his second coup and returned to power as the Chairman of the Provisional National Defence Council, comprised of both civilians and military officers. Expressing national-populist sentiments and promising a return to democracy, the regime managed to postpone national elections until 1992 when Rawlings was elected President by a large margin.

Like his Argentine counterpart Carlos Menem, however, Rawlings gave up his national-populist stance when he realized the depleted status of his country's foreign exchange reserves. Accepting IMF-imposed conditionalities – cutting state expenditures, promoting private sector development, attracting foreign investment, reducing capital controls and trade barriers, liberalizing exchange rates, and supporting joint ventures between foreign and local investors – in exchange for much-needed loans, Rawlings embarked in 1983 on his neoliberal Economic Recovery Programme. Encountering serious resistance from the trade unions and various student movements, Ghana's strongman

15. Jeremiah (Jerry) Rawlings (1947–); Ghana's Head of State (1979; 1981–93); President of Ghana (1993–2001)

tightened his authoritarian grip on the political Left to carry out his free-market reforms.

Central to Rawlings's economic vision was the neoliberal idea that the transformation of the public sector into vibrant private companies would create thousands of new jobs, raise incomes, and increase the flow of foreign investment to further accelerate the privatization of state-owned enterprises. In addition to severely cutting welfare programmes and reducing food subsidies, he decreased tariffs on imports and deregulated his country's banking system. As in the Latin American countries we examined, the results of these policies were mixed at best. Inflation was substantially reduced from well over 100% in the early 1980s to about 30% by the end of the decade. At the same time, unemployment and the number of people living in poverty increased significantly. The principal beneficiaries of currency devaluations were large landowners and foreign investors involved in the production and export of Ghana's cash crops such as cocoa and wood products as well as mining in precious metals such as gold.

By contrast, however, urban workers suffered as the prices on import goods and export commodities skyrocketed while their wages increased only modestly. Likewise, the government's removal on capital controls advantaged global investors, foreign creditors, and transnational corporations who were now free to extract their profits with only minimal tax reductions. Trade liberalization lifted both import and export-oriented businesses, particularly those with strong ties to foreign capital investment. The privatization of

Gold mining in Ghana in the era of neoliberalism

At first glance, the privatization of the gold mines in Ghana in the 1980s and 1990s appears to have achieved what neoliberal economists had predicted. It attracted large amounts of foreign direct investment and led to a dramatic rise in production from

300,000 ounces in 1985 to 2,336,000 ounces in 2001. By the mid-2000s, gold had actually replaced cocoa as Ghana's main export. Yet, a balanced 2003 World Bank report also reveals the negative effects of privatization. First, capital-intensive mining by foreign firms requires expensive imported materials and machines and thus produces only modest amounts of net foreign exchange for Ghana. Second, tax revenues are slight due to the various tax incentives offered to foreign corporations. Third, modern surface mining techniques have drastically reduced the number of labourers needed to extract the gold, thus creating only few new jobs for the Ghanaian workforce. Fourth, large-scale mining competes with agriculture for arable land, thus negatively impacting the viability of local economies. Finally, gold mining has long been implicated in serious cases of environmental degradation.

Source: James Ferguson, *Global Shadow: Africa in the Neoliberal World Order* (Durham and London: Duke University Press, 2006), pp. 36–7

state-owned industries served the interests of domestic and international investors who were in the position of acquiring these industries at rock-bottom prices. Higher prices for cocoa beans and other cash crops translated into higher profits for large landowning farmers while burdening small farmers and agricultural workers.

For most of the 1990s, Ghana enjoyed dramatic increases in foreign investment averaging $133 million a year, and gold production climbed by nearly 40%. During this period the country's financial markets were performing well, though most Ghanaians could not afford to purchase stocks or bonds. But the Ghanaian economy fell into crisis in 1999–2000 when cocoa and gold prices plummeted while the prices for imported petroleum dramatically increased. Once again having to rely on external loans, the government was forced to borrow at exorbitant interest rates, thus pushing up inflation as high as 40% and devaluing the currency by 30%. More recently, Ghana's

Heavily Indebted Poor Countries (HIPCs)

HIPCs are comprised of about 40 developing nations with high levels of poverty and indebtedness. They are eligible for special assistance from the IMF and the World Bank, which provide them with debt relief and low-interest loans to reduce external debt repayments to sustainable levels. But this form of assistance depends on the ability of national governments to meet a clearly defined range of economic management and performance targets.

Ghana's human development index 2005				
HDI value	Life expectancy at birth (years)	Adult literacy rate (% ages 15 and older)	Combined primary, secondary and tertiary gross enrolment ratio (%)	GDP per capita (PPP US$)
1. Iceland (0.968)	1. Japan (82.3)	1. Georgia (100.0)	1. Australia (113.0)	1. Luxembourg (60,228)
133. Bhutan (0.579)	135. Timor-Leste (59.7)	115. Sudan (60.9)	144. Congo (51.4)	124. Cambodia (2,727)
134. Comoros (0.561)	136. Haiti (59.5)	116. Burundi (59.3)	145. Rwanda (50.9)	125. Papua New Guinea (2,563)
135. Ghana (0.553)	*137. Ghana (59.1)*	*117. Ghana (57.9)*	*146. Ghana (50.7)*	*126. Ghana (2,480)*
136. Pakistan (0.551)	138. Gambia (58.8)	118. Papua New Guinea (57.3)	147. Benin (50.7)	127. Pakistan (2,370)
137. Mauritania (0.550)	139. Madagascar (58.4)	119. Yemen (54.1)	148. Tanzania (United Republic of) (50.4)	128. Angola (2,335)
177. Sierra Leone (0.336)	177. Zambia (40.5)	139. Burkina Faso (23.6)	172. Niger (22.7)	174. Malawi (667)

H. Ghana's Human Development Index, 2005
The Human Development index is used by the United Nations Development Program. It aims to provide a more comprehensive measure of the 'human condition' and experience of people living in a country than is typically offered by standard measures of a national income such as GDP/Capita alone. Designed in accordance with the proposition that 'people are the real wealth of nations', indicators such as life expectancy, adult literacy, and GDP (measured in terms of purchasing power) are ranked and compared across nations.

Source: http://hdr.undp.org/en/

democratically elected President John Kufuor has sought to court foreign investment with little success. Faced with rampant inflation and economic collapse in February 2008, he accepted an arrangement with the IMF and World Bank that placed Ghana under the protection of the Heavily Indebted Poor Countries programme.

The President explained his decision to the Ghanaian people, stating that the arrangement would provide the country with desperately needed partial cancellation of its $5.8 billion foreign debt. Kufuor argued that these measures, combined with expected new revenues from recent petroleum finds in the country, would help put Ghana's economy back on track. Moreover, he asserted that the relief offered by the HIPC programme would allow his government to invest the savings in social welfare. Whatever the future holds for Ghana, it seems clear that its economy has failed to perform according to the expectations and standards set for it by the IMF and the World Bank several decades ago.

Concluding remarks

Our examination of the impact of the Washington Consensus on Latin America and Africa revealed the existence of similar patterns and outcomes. From the perspective of the IMF or the World Bank, market-oriented reform in this region was needed to produce sustained economic growth and thus lift millions of people out of poverty. To that end, they linked their financial assistance to structural adjustment programmes anchored in one-size-fits-all economic prescriptions. Even if we were to set aside possible objections to neoliberal doctrine itself, it would seem obvious that anyone seeking structural reforms to 'make markets work' might consider that not all markets 'work' in exactly the same way and according to the same rules. And there is also the problem of applying rigid formulas in different social contexts. The neoliberal remedies applied to Latin America and Africa are microeconomic strategies based on specific social, political, and cultural assumptions. Neoliberal principles of 'private entrepreneurship' or 'profit-maximization' are not necessarily universal norms that can be simply dropped on the 'developing world'. Indeed, it makes little sense to assume that the policy prescriptions of the Washington Consensus could be implemented by fiat in the course of a decade or two. To their credit, however, international economic institutions like the IMF or the World Bank have begun to rethink their time-worn strategies. In addition, the current global financial crisis has forced political leaders in both the North and the South to question the neoliberal design and practices of the world's economic architecture.

Chapter 6
Crises of neoliberalism: the 2000s and beyond

As we have seen in the previous chapters, by the end of the Roaring Nineties, neoliberalism in its various permutations and modifications had successfully spread to most parts of the world. Its powerful advocates in the West had employed the compelling narrative of inevitable market globalization to convince people that the liberalization of trade and minimally regulated markets will result in high economic growth and dramatic improvement in living conditions worldwide. And yet, in addition to relying on this potent arsenal of ideological representation, the spread of neoliberalism required at times the co-option of local elites, often by means of indirect coercion through international economic institutions like the IMF and the World Bank, which insisted on the adoption of structural adjustment programmes in return for much-needed loans.

Despite its undeniable achievements in overcoming the 'stagflation' years of the late 1970s, for example, neoliberalism created both winners and losers in the globalizing economy. Its uneven distribution of material benefits sparked serious challenges and crises such as the 1994 uprising of the Zapatista Army of National Liberation against the Washington Consensus or the 1997–8 Asian Financial Crisis that was soon followed by economic crashes in Russia and Brazil. A year later, millions of ordinary people around the world took to the streets in Seattle,

Washington, DC, Davos, Salzburg, Melbourne, Manila, Prague, Gothenburg, and other world cities to protest widening global inequalities and sweatshop working conditions they ascribed to the neoliberal trade and development agenda designed by the IMF and the World Trade Organization. The massive protests at the August 2001 G-8 Summit in Genoa, Italy, gave a clear indication that millions of people around the world had rejected the neoliberal dream of a single global market fuelled by ceaseless consumerist desires. Confronting the market-globalist juggernaut, these 'alter-globalization' protestors had successfully coalesced into a sizeable 'global justice movement'. Establishing the World Social Forum in Brazil as their annual meeting place, these activists drew up an anti-neoliberal Charter of Principles anchored in their conviction that 'another world' was possible.

Reacting to rising cultural and ethnic tensions in an increasingly globalized world, nationalist forces on the political Right were also gathering strength in the late 1990s. Castigating market globalism for the breakdown of community and traditional ways of life, they also bemoaned the displacement of small farmers and increased levels of immigration in their countries. Populist political leaders such as Patrick Buchanan in the United States, Jörg Haider in Austria, Jean-Marie Le Pen in France, Christoph Blocher in Switzerland, Gianfranco Fini in Italy, Pauline Hanson in Australia, and Winston Peters in New Zealand expressed their opposition to neoliberal 'market fundamentalism'. They also denounced free trade, the increasing power of global investors, and the 'outsourcing' of domestic manufacturing jobs as 'unpatriotic' practices that had contributed to falling living standards and moral decline. In the global South, similar voices of national-populism blamed neoliberal globalization and the expansion of American power for economic decline and cultural decay. Venezuelan President Hugo Chávez, for example, pledged to protect his nation from such 'neoliberal internationalism'.

Ridiculing what they considered to be the 'outdated protectionism' and 'parochialism' of their critics on the Right, second-wave neoliberals reacted especially strongly to their challengers on the Left. Claiming to act in a purely defensive manner, political leaders began to rely more heavily on the coercive powers of the state to keep such 'anti-globalizers' in check. In addition, mainstream media pushed the stereotype of Molotov-cocktail-throwing anarchists on often ill-informed TV audiences. These attempts to stabilize the neoliberal model by means of generating fear were increasingly reflected in public discourse. For example, globalizing markets were now portrayed as requiring protection against violent and irrational protesters. It seemed that the allegedly 'inevitable' evolution of market globalism now needed to be helped along by strong law enforcement measures that would beat back the 'enemies of democracy and the free market'.

But the fear factor did not come into full play until the traumatic events of 11 September 2001, when radical forces of jihadist globalism attacked what they considered to be the 'godless' and 'materialistic' symbols of the world's most neoliberal society. By the time al-Qaeda launched its heinous attacks, the link between political violence and anti-globalization demonstrators was already so firmly anchored in the public mind that a number of commentators in the global North immediately named such 'radical elements' as the prime suspects. When it became clear that the terrorist network led by Osama Bin Laden and Ayman al-Zawahiri was behind these horrendous atrocities, the negative stereotype of the chaotic global justice movement was quickly eclipsed by the menacing image of Islamist extremists organized in clandestine cells around the world. As neoliberalism clashed head-on with global jihadism, President George W. Bush and Prime Minster Tony Blair turned the security crisis afflicting the world into an opportunity for extending the hegemony of neoliberalism on new terms. Thus, in the first years of the 21st century, neoliberal market language merged with a neoconservative security agenda. Countries were told in no uncertain terms to stand with the leader of global neoliberalism – the United States of America – on the side of 'civilization' against the forces of terrorism or face the consequences of their bad choice. To be 'civilized' meant not only to embrace American-style democracy and free markets, but also to refrain from criticizing American foreign policy. Countries like France, Germany, and Russia, who opposed the 2003 invasion of Iraq, paid a high economic price for their insubordination: the vengeful Bush administration simply cut them out of lucrative business contracts for rebuilding a devastated country.

Initially confined to Afghanistan and Iraq, the so-called 'Global War on Terror' soon expanded to other parts of the world, like Somalia and Indonesia, and, more recently, back to Afghanistan and Pakistan. At the same time, however, al-Qaeda-style terrorist cells continued their jihadist campaign. Their simple ideological imperative – rebuild a unified global *umma* (Islamic community of believers) through global *jihad* against 'global unbelief' – resonated with the dynamics of a globalizing world. It held a special appeal for alienated Muslim youths between the ages of 15 and 25 who lived for sustained periods of time in the West, especially in Europe. Responsible for the most spectacular terrorist operations executed between 11 September 2001, and the London bombings of 7 July 2005, these latest recruits shared Bin Laden's conviction that the 'destructive, usurious global economy' constituted a deliberate weapon in the hands of the West to 'impose unbelief and humiliation' on the Islamic world.

Osama Bin Laden's chilling cost–benefit analysis of the 9/11 attacks

Al-Qaeda spent $500,000 on the 11 September attacks, while America lost more than $500 billion, at the lowest estimate, in the event and its aftermath. That makes a million American dollars for every al-Qaeda dollar, by the grace of Gold Almighty. This is in addition to the fact that it lost an enormous number of jobs – and as for the federal deficit, it made record losses, estimated over a trillion dollars. Still more serious for America was the fact that the *mujahideen* forced Bush to resort to an emergency budget in order to continue fighting in Afghanistan and Iraq. This shows the success of our plan to bleed America to the point of bankruptcy, with God's will.

Source: Osama Bin Laden, 'The Towers of Lebanon' (29 October 2004), in *Messages to the World: The Statements of Osama Bin Laden*, edited by Bruce Lawrence and translated by James Howarth (London: Verso, 2005), p. 242

In his videotaped message delivered in September 2007, Bin Laden unleashed further verbal broadsides against neoliberalism and the 'corrupt American political system'. He linked the Bush administration's involvement in Iraq to transnational corporate interests that held the world hostage to their all-out scramble for war-related profits. Charging 'the capitalist system' with seeking 'to turn the entire world into a fiefdom of the major corporations under the label of 'globalization', Bin Laden articulated a criticism of neoliberal market globalism that was shared by opponents of neoliberalism across the Left/Right ideological divide – though the principles and horrific methods of al-Qaeda have been unambiguously denounced by the leaders of the global justice movement. Hence, when the collapse of the American real-estate market in late 2007 triggered what came to be known as the 'global financial crisis', neoliberalism had already been subjected to sustained criticism from the combined forces of the radical Left and Right for nearly a decade.

The global financial crisis: causes and consequences

During the 1980s and 1990s, US mortgage markets were stimulated as three successive neoliberal governments raised borrowing limits and reduced asset requirements for loans. Starting with the Reagan administration, these governments contributed to the significant deregulation of the US financial services industry. Perhaps the most important initiative in this regard was the assault on the Glass-Steagall Act, which was signed into law by President Roosevelt in 1933 to prohibit commercial banks from engaging in investment activities on Wall Street. After all, the 1929 Crash and the ensuing Great Depression had exposed the dangers of the savings and loan industry partaking in the speculative frenzy on Wall Street, which had ultimately led to the bankruptcy of many commercial banks and the loss of their customers' assets.

In the spring of 1987, the Federal Reserve Board voted to ease some of the Glass-Steagall regulations, arguing that three effective checks on corporate speculation had emerged since the dark days of the Great Depression that made a return of such a large-scale economic crisis highly unlikely: (1) an 'effective' Securities Exchange Commission (SEC); (2) the higher sophistication level of most investors; (3) independent rating credit agencies like Moody's Investors Services that delivered accurate and reliable information to investors. By the early 1990s, large commercial banks such as J. P. Morgan, Citicorp, and Chase Manhattan had received permission from the Federal Reserve to underwrite securities. In 1996, the Reserve Board under the leadership of Chairman Alan Greenspan ruled to allow bank holding companies to own investment bank affiliates with up to 25% of their business in securities underwriting. In 1999, Congress voted to repeal Glass-Steagall with President Clinton signing the new legislation, thus removing any restrictions on commercial bank ownership of investment banks.

This series of neoliberal deregulations resulted in a frenzy of mergers that gave birth to huge financial-services conglomerates eager to plunge into securities ventures in areas that were not necessarily part of their underlying business. Derivatives, financial futures, credit default swaps, and related instruments became extremely popular when new computer-based mathematical models suggested more secure ways of managing the risk involved in buying an asset in the future at a price agreed to in the present. Relying far less on savings deposits, financial institutions borrowed from each other and sold these loans as securities, thus passing the risk on to investors into these securities. Other 'innovative' financial instruments such as 'hedge funds' leveraged with borrowed funds fuelled a variety of speculative activities, including full-scale attacks on national currencies. Billions of investment dollars flowed into complex 'residential mortgage-backed securities' that promised investors up to 25% return on equity.

Assured by Chairman Greenspan's monetarist policies of keeping interest rates low and credit flowing, investment banks eventually expanded their search for capital by buying risky 'subprime' loans from mortgage brokers who, lured by the promise of big commissions, were accepting applications for housing mortgages with little or no down payment and without credit checks. Increasingly popular in the United States, most of these loans were adjustable-rate mortgages tied to fluctuations of short-term interest rates. Investment banks snapped up these high-risk loans knowing that they could resell these assets – and thus the risk involved – by bundling them into composite securities no longer subject to government regulation. Indeed, one of the most complex of these 'innovative' instruments of securitization – so-called 'collateralized debt obligations' – often hid the problematic loans by bundling them together with lower-risk assets and reselling them to unsuspecting investors.

But why, given the poor quality of collateral, did individual and institutional investors continue to buy these mortgage-backed securities? One can think of three principal reasons. First, as noted above, esoteric forms of securities often concealed the degree of risk involved, and investors failed to grasp the complexity of these new investment funds. Second, investors relied on the excellent reputation of such financial giants as Bank of America or Citicorp. Third, they trusted the positive credit ratings reports issued by Standard and Poor's or Moody's, failing to see how these firms were themselves implicated in the expanding speculative bubble. Seeking to maximize their profits, these credit ratings giants had a vested interest in the growth of securities markets and thus took an extremely rosy view of the inherent risks.

Wall Street's 'innovative investment' toolbox defined

Derivatives: A financial asset whose value is derived from that of other assets.

Securities: Assets such as stocks and bonds to be traded on a secondary market. Securities derivatives include future contracts, options, and mutual funds.

Securitization: The bundling of thousands of loans and mortgages into huge repackaged and revalued portfolios to be sliced up and sold to investors.

Credit default swaps: Derivatives allowing buyers to make payments to the seller in order to receive a one-time payoff in case a specified third party defaults on its debt to the seller.

Hedge funds: Largely unregulated investment funds open to a limited number of professional and wealthy investors who engage in a broad range of investments including shares, debts, and commodities.

To hedge: Attempt to forestall loss on an investment by using such techniques as short-selling.

Short sale: The sale of securities to a seller who does not own these assets (and thus must borrow against them) but intends to reacquire them at a future date at a lower price. If the price of the security drops, the seller profits due to the difference between the price of the shares sold and the price of the shares bought to pay back the borrowed shares.

Leverage: The use of credit to improve investors' speculative purchase power and thus possibly increase the rate of return on their investment.

Arbitrage: The simultaneous buying and selling of securities in different markets in order to profit from price differences in these markets.

The high yields flowing from these new securities funds attracted more and more investors around the world, thus rapidly globalizing more than a trillion US dollars worth of what came to be known as 'toxic assets'. In mid-2007, however, the financial steamroller finally ran out of fuel when seriously overvalued American real estate began to drop and foreclosures shot up dramatically. Investors finally realized the serious risks attached to the securities market and lost confidence. Consequently, the value of securitized mortgage funds fell and banks desperately tried in vain to somehow eliminate the debts showing on their balance sheets.

Some of the largest and most venerable financial institutions, insurance companies, and government-sponsored underwriters of mortgages such as Lehman Brothers, Bear Stearns, Merrill Lynch, Goldman Sachs, AIG, Citicorp, J. P. Morgan Chase, IndyMac Bank, Morgan Stanley, Fannie Mae, and Freddie Mac – to name but a few – either declared bankruptcy or had to be rescued by what amounted to America's most spectacular 'nationalization' drive since the Great Depression. Ironically, the conservative Bush administration championed the purchase of up to $700 billion in distressed mortgage securities in return for a government share in the businesses involved. Britain and most other industrialized countries followed suit with their own multi-billion bailout packages, hoping that such massive injections of capital into ailing financial markets would help to prop up financial institutions deemed 'too large to be allowed to fail'. But these generous rescue packages allowed large financial conglomerates to lose even more

Chief Executive	Corporation	Total Compensation Package for 2008 (In Millions of US Dollars)	Daily Compensation (approx.)
Sanjay K. Jha	Motorola	$104.4	$285,000
Lawrence J. Ellison	Oracle	$84.6	$233,000
Robert A. Iger	Walt Disney	$51.1	$140,000
Kenneth I. Chenault	American Express	$42.8	$118,000
Vikram S. Pandit	Citigroup	$38.2	$105,000
Mark V. Hurd	Hewlett-Packard	$34.0	$93,000
Jack A. Fusco	Calpine	$32.7	$90,000
Rupert K. Murdoch	News Corp.	$30.1	$82,000
David M. Cote	Honeywell Int'l.	$28.7	$80,000
Alan G. Lafley	Procter & Gamble	$25.6	$71,000

I. 2008 compensation packages (salary, bonuses, and stock options) of the top-ten US CEOs

Source: *New York Times*, 5 April, 2009

money without having to declare bankruptcy. The cost passed on to the world's taxpayers is truly staggering: future generations will have to repay trillions of dollars used for financing these bailout packages.

The great Icelandic meltdown

In the early 2000s, the government of the small nation of Iceland liberalized its three major banks, thus allowing them to acquire massive capital from the global credit markets. Offering extremely high interest on regular savings accounts, Iceland's banks attracted deposits worth nearly two billion dollars from investors in Europe. However, when the global financial crisis put an end to easy credit and forced the devaluation of the Icelandic krona, the country's banks found themselves unable to finance their debts, many of which were denominated in foreign currencies. Depositors tried to access their money but the banks had insufficient reserves to cover the withdrawals and proceeded to freeze many bank accounts. Left with no choice but to re-nationalize the banks in October 2008, Iceland's government turned to the IMF for a ten-billion-dollar loan in order to avoid economic collapse.

However, one of the major consequences of the failing financial system was that banks trying to rebuild their capital base could hardly afford to keep lending large amounts of money. The flow of credit froze to a trickle and businesses and individuals who relied on credit found it much more difficult to obtain. This credit

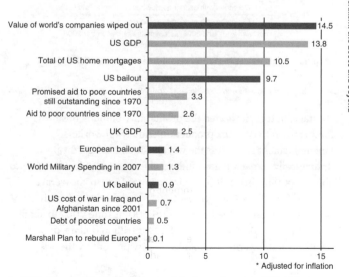

J. **Global financial crisis: losses and bailouts for US and European countries in context**

Source: www.globalissues.org, February 2009

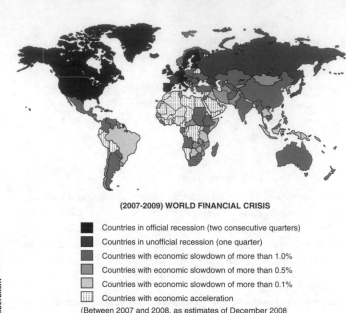

(2007-2009) WORLD FINANCIAL CRISIS

■ Countries in official recession (two consecutive quarters)
■ Countries in unofficial recession (one quarter)
■ Countries with economic slowdown of more than 1.0%
■ Countries with economic slowdown of more than 0.5%
□ Countries with economic slowdown of more than 0.1%
▦ Countries with economic acceleration
(Between 2007 and 2008, as estimates of December 2008
by the International Monetary Fund)

Map 2. Countries falling into recession as a result of the global financial crisis

Source: http://en.wikipedia.org/wiki/File:2007-2009_World_Financial_Crisis.svg#file

shortage, in turn, impacted the profitability of many businesses, forcing them to cut back production and lay off workers. Unemployment shot up as the world's stock markets dropped dramatically. Japan's Nikkei index fell from 18,000 in July 2007 to about 8,000 in early 2009; the Dow Jones Industrial Average dropped from 14,000 in October 2007 to below 7,000 in early 2009; and the Paris CAC 40 fell from over 6,000 in June 2007 to about 3,000 in early 2009. By early 2009, 14.3 trillion dollars, or 33% of the value of the world's companies, was wiped out by the crisis.

Industrial output in 2008 declined by 31% in Japan, 26% in Korea, 16% in Russia, 15% in Brazil, 14% in Italy, and 12% in Germany. One after another, the economies of countries around the world dipped into recession. The World Bank's March 2009 forecast suggested that both the global economy and the volume of foreign trade would shrink for the first time since World War II. The report noted that the developing world would be especially hard hit, facing a financial shortfall of $700 billion by the end of 2010. The International Labour Organization predicted that the crisis would wipe out at least 20 million jobs by the end of 2009, bringing global unemployment to an unprecedented number of over 200 million. Zagat's Hotels, Resorts and Spas Survey suggested that business travel in 2009 might fall by as much as 30%. In short, the global *financial* crisis has turned into a global *economic* crisis.

The end of neoliberalism?

By early 2009, economic experts around the world agreed that the global economy was in the midst of a recession that threatened to snowball into another Great Depression. Although some of these commentators highlighted the role of 'greedy Wall Street bankers' in bringing about this crisis, most blamed global financial elites for adhering to a neoliberal dogmatism. Political leaders both on the Left and the Right not only openly questioned the tenets of neoliberalism, but also argued in favour of greater regulatory oversight by national and global institutions. Former Federal Reserve Chairman Alan Greenspan admitted in front of the US Congressional Committee on Oversight and Government Reform that his neoliberal ideology was no longer working. Even prominent conservatives writing for large audiences like *New York Times* columnist David Brooks conceded that free markets were not self-regulating and perfectly efficient and people were not always good guardians of their own self-interest. But perhaps the most comprehensive and sophisticated criticism of the neoliberal model came in March 2009 in the form of a 65-page United Nations Conference on Trade and Development (UNCTAD) Report, titled 'The Global Economic Crisis: Systematic Failures and Multilateral Remedies'.

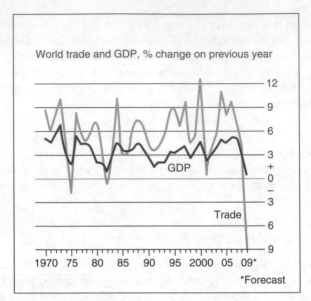

K. The collapse of world trade

Source: *The Economist*, print edition, 26 March, 2009

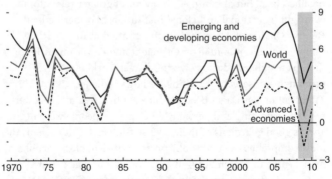

L. The contraction of the world economy

Source: www.imf.org/external/pubs/ft/weo/2009/update/01/index.htm

132

World leaders criticize neoliberalism in response to the global economic crisis

'*Laissez-faire* is finished.'

French President Nicolas Sarkozy, January 2009

'The global financial crisis is a crisis which is simultaneously individual, national, and global. It is a crisis of both the developed and developing world. It is a crisis which is at once institutional, intellectual, and ideological. It has called into question the prevailing neoliberal economic orthodoxy of the past 30 years – the orthodoxy that has underpinned the national and global regulatory frameworks that have so spectacularly failed to prevent the economic mayhem which has been visited upon us.'

Australian Prime Minister Kevin Rudd, February 2009

'The old world of the Washington Consensus is over.'

British Prime Minister Gordon Brown, April 2009

The UNCTAD Report contains four key messages. First, it emphasizes that 'market fundamentalist *laissez-faire*' of the last two decades had dramatically failed the test on real-world application. Financial deregulation had created the build-up of huge financial risks whose unwinding had pushed the global economy into debt deflation that, ultimately, could only be countered by government debt inflation. Second, 'blind faith in the efficiency of deregulated financial markets' and the absence of a cooperative financial and monetary system had created an illusion of risk-free profits and licensed profligacy through speculative finance. Third, the growing role of financial conglomerates on commodities and derivatives had led to extreme volatility and the emergence of speculative commodity 'bubbles' such as the US housing bubble. Finally, similar to the 1997–8 Asian Crisis, the absence of a cooperative international system to manage exchange rate fluctuations had facilitated rampant currency speculations and increased global imbalances, thus bringing a number of countries to the verge of default.

Aside from sounding like the obituary of neoliberalism, the UNCTAD Report also suggested three constructive remedies: (1) comprehensive re-regulation of the global financial system with the world's governments working in unison to achieve this goal; (2) government–private sector cooperation to stimulate economic growth; (3) developing countries should no longer be subjected to the kind of neoliberal logic that caused the current crisis in the first place. Indeed, less than a month after the publication of the UNCTAD Report the heads of state of the G-20 Summit met in London to agree on a common economic strategy. As British Prime Minister Gordon Brown put it, this meeting in response to the global financial crisis created an 'historic opportunity' to establish a 'new world order'. After initial tensions between a faction led by President Nicolas Sarkozy and Chancellor Angela Merkel, who favoured stronger regulatory controls on a global scale, and one headed by President Obama, Prime Minister Brown, and Japanese Prime Minster Taro Aso, who emphasized the importance of further stimulus packages, the G-20 leaders succeeded in hammering out the general principles in a joint communiqué published on 2 April 2009.

Six key points of the G-20 agreements

- Reform of the global banking system, with controls on hedge funds, better accounting standards, tighter rules for credit-rating agencies, curbs on excessive executive remuneration, and the naming-and-shaming of tax havens that fail to share information.

- A new Financial Stability Board will be set up to work with the IMF to ensure cooperation across borders and provide an early warning mechanism for the financial system. Its members will include finance ministries, regulators, and central banks from G-20 countries.

- A $1.1 trillion package to supplement the $5 trillion stimulus to the global economy by individual countries. $750 billion – the lion's share of the 1.1 trillion – will go to the IMF, the rest to the World Bank and other institutions to restore credit, jobs and increase lending to vulnerable countries.

- More power for leading developing countries such as China and India to determine IMF and World Bank policies.

- $200 billion of trade finance over 2009–10 to help reverse the decline in world trade.

- A pledge that part of the fiscal stimulus, including the sale of gold by the World Bank to raise $6 billion, will be used to help the poorest nations as well as to create 'green' jobs.

Source: The Guardian, 2 April 2009

The agreement was hailed by business leaders as a crucial step in repairing the world's financial infrastructure, while critics on the Left assailed the moderate character of the reforms, the lack of specifics, and the absence of concrete measures to combat global climate change. Moreover, the G-20 communiqué left the required reforms of the banking system in the hands of each national government to act on a 'case-by-case' basis. Unsurprisingly, many national banking executives immediately resisted such measures, arguing that the pendulum of regulation would swing too heavily against the financial sector. In addition, the new Financial Stability Board was not given any binding enforcement power. Rather, its main activities were limited to advising members, monitoring regulations, and collaborating with the IMF to create early-warning mechanisms aimed at preventing the next financial crisis. Finally, although it was obvious that the G-20 agreements gave the IMF a pivotal role in the desired reform process, it was not entirely clear how quickly and thoroughly this newly empowered institution would be able to wean itself from its old neoliberal logic. Thus, we can end by saying that while it would be premature to pronounce neoliberalism dead, it would be equally foolish to deny that a crisis-ridden world has begun to flirt once again with Keynesian principles.

Conclusion

Having reached the end of our journey through the diverse landscapes of neoliberalism, let us briefly summarize our findings. Arguing that neoliberalism functions as an ideology, a mode of governance, and a policy package emphasizing the pivotal role of free markets and private enterprise, we noted that it swept the world in two successive waves, starting in the 1980s in the United Kingdom and the United States. Boldly putting the economic ideas of Hayek and Friedman into practice, in the process, Reaganomics and Thatcherism succeeded in shattering the Keynesian paradigm that had dominated economic theory and practice since the dark years of the Great Depression. Although these two first-wave variants developed their own set of policy preferences, they shared a common desire to reshape their respective societies according to the neoliberal D[eregulation]-L[iberalization]-P[rivatization] formula.

During the Roaring Nineties, second-wave neoliberalisms adopted by 'centre-left' politicians such as Bill Clinton and Tony Blair sought to balance their free-market thinking with some sense of social responsibility and community. At the same time, however, they utilized the 'soft power' of the IMF and the World Bank to export the 'Washington Consensus' to the rest of the world. Their firm commitment to a global economy fuelled by transnational trade resulted in a number of regional free-trade agreements. In addition, the newly created WTO became the powerful watchdog and enforcer of market globalism's liberalization agenda. By the turn of the century, however, a series of challenges to the hegemony of neoliberalism managed to make their mark, but failed to bring about fundamental change. It was left to the global economic crisis of 2008–9 (continuing, perhaps, beyond these two years) to destabilize the unrivalled reign of neoliberalism precisely 30 years after Margaret Thatcher's ascent to the office of Prime Minister.

While it is clear that first-wave and even second-wave manifestations have had their day, it is far from certain that neoliberalism as such has exited the world stage for good. As we emphasized throughout this book, neoliberalism comes in many varieties which have proven to be extremely adaptable to specific social contexts. Moreover, the preliminary agreements struck among G-20 leaders at the 2009 London Summit to apply some Keynesian remedies to the ailing global economy might turn out to be unsustainable in the long run. Although it looks as though free-market fundamentalism has been relegated to the dustbin of history, the second pillar of neoliberalism – free trade – is not only still standing but has been reaffirmed as 'indispensable' by political and economic elites around the world. It is entirely conceivable that a possible economic recovery as soon as 2010 or 2011 might once again embolden those very neoliberal voices who, for the moment, have been silenced by the current calamity. On the other hand, if the crisis continues, or even deepens, the calls for more radical surgery will undoubtedly become louder, possibly creating enough pressure to usher in a new era of globally controlled capitalism. Thus, both third-wave neoliberalism (of a more moderate kind than its two predecessors) and a global new deal (built on Keynesian principles) are distinct possibilities for the second decade of the 21st century.

References

As one would expect, there is an extensive literature on neoliberalism and related themes, but most of these books and articles are not easily accessible to those who are just setting out to acquire some knowledge of the subject. Having digested the contents of the present introduction, however, most readers will find themselves equipped to move on to some of the academic works listed below. Indeed, some of these writings have influenced the arguments made in the present volume. Following the overall organization of Oxford's Very Short Introduction series, however, we have kept direct quotations to a minimum and indicated the source at the bottom of the text boxes. Still, we wish to acknowledge our intellectual debt to the authors below, whose influence on the arguments of this book is not always obvious from the text.

Preface

For an excellent discussion of the origin and various uses of the term 'neoliberalism' in academic social science literature, see Taylor C. Boas and Jordan Gans-Morse, 'Neoliberalism: From New Liberal Philosophy to Anti-Liberal Slogan', *Studies in Comparative International Development* 44.2 (June 2009), pp. 137–61.

Chapter 1

Perhaps the most comprehensive survey of neoliberalism available to an academic audience today is David Harvey, *A Brief History of*

Neoliberalism (Oxford University Press, 2005). A critical account of the origins, workings, and influence of the Washington Consensus can be found in Andrew Gamble, *The Global Gamble: Washington's Faustian Bid for World Dominance* (Verso, 1999). For a collection of critical essays on neoliberalism from a Left perspective, see Alfredo Saad-Filho and Deborah Johnston, *Neoliberalism: A Critical Reader* (Pluto Press, 2005). For an ideologically more balanced anthology, see Ravi K. Roy, Arthur T. Denzau, and Thomas D. Willett (eds.), *Neoliberalism: National and Regional Experiments with Global Ideas* (Routledge, 2006).

Accessible books on classical liberalism include: Robert L. Heilbroner, *The Worldly Philosophers: The Lives, Times, and Ideas of the Great Economic Thinkers* (Touchstone, 1999); Jerry Z. Muller, *The Mind and the Market: Capitalism in Modern European Thought* (Alfred A. Knopf, 2002); and Karl Polanyi, *The Great Transformation: The Political and Economic Origins of our Time* (Beacon Press, 2001 [1944]). A representative collection of essays on libertarianism can be found in David Boaz (ed.), *Libertarianism: A Primer* (The Free Press, 1998). For a brilliant economic history of the 20th century, see Jeffry A. Frieden, *Global Capitalism: Its Fall and Rise in the Twentieth Century* (W. W. Norton, 2006).

For materials related to the economic ideas of John Maynard Keynes, Friedrich von Hayek, and Milton Friedman, see Peter A. Hall (ed.), *The Political Power of Economic Ideas: Keynesianism across Nations* (Princeton University Press, 1989); Mark Blyth, *Great Transformations: Economic Ideas and Institutional Change in the Twentieth Century* (Cambridge University Press, 2002); Kenneth R. Hoover, *Economics as Ideology: Keynes, Laski, Hayek and the Creation of Contemporary Politics* (Rowman and Littlefield, 2003); Friedrich A. Hayek, *The Road to Serfdom* (University of Chicago Press, 1994 [1944]); Alan Ebenstein, *Hayek's Journey: The Mind of Friedrich Hayek* (Palgrave Macmillan, 2003); and Milton Friedman, *Capitalism and Freedom* (University of Chicago Press, 2002 [1962]).

For representative surveys and histories of political ideologies, see Michael Freeden, *Ideology: A Very Short Introduction* (Oxford University Press, 2009); Lyman Sargent Tower, *Contemporary Political Ideologies: A Comparative Analysis*, 14th edn. (Wadsworth, 2009); and Manfred B. Steger, *The Rise of the Global Imaginary: Political Ideologies from the French Revolution to the Global War on Terror* (Oxford University Press, 2008).

The transcript of Barack Obama's 2009 Inauguration Address is available at: http://www.nytimes.com/2009/01/20/us/politics/20text-obama.html

Chapter 2

For further readings on Reaganomics and Thatcherism, see William A. Niskanen, *Reaganomics: An Insider's Account of the Policies and the People* (Oxford University Press, 1988); David A. Stockman, *The Triumph of Politics: How the Reagan Revolution Failed* (Harper & Row, 1986); Michael J. Boskin, *Reagan and the Economy: The Successes, Failures, and Unfinished Agenda* (ICS Press, 1987); Anandi P. Sahu and Ronald L. Tracy (eds.), *The Economic Legacy of the Reagan Years: Euphoria or Chaos?* (Praeger, 1991); Stuart Hall and Martin Jacques (eds.), *The Politics of Thatcherism* (Lawrence and Wisehart, 1983); Sven Steinmo, *Taxation and Democracy: Swedish, British and American Approaches to Financing the Modern State* (Yale University Press, 1993); Richard Heffernan, *New Labour and Thatcherism: Political Change in Britain* (St Martin's Press, 2000); Eric J. Evans, *Thatcher and Thatcherism* (Routledge, 2004); Ravi K. Roy, *Fiscal Policy from Reagan to Blair: The Left Veers Right* (Routledge, 2004); Earl A. Reitan, *The Thatcher Revolution: Margaret Thatcher, John Major, Tony Blair, and the Transformation of Modern Britain, 1979–2001* (Rowman & Littlefield, 2003); and Monica Prasad, *The Politics of Free Markets: The Rise of Neoliberal Economic Policies in Britain, France, Germany, and the United States* (University of Chicago Press, 2006).

For an enlightening reassessment of Reagan's foreign policy at the end of the Cold War, see Norman A. Graebner, Richard Dean Burns, and Joseph M. Siracusa, *Reagan, Bush, Gorbachev: Revisiting the End of the Cold War* (Praeger Security International, 2008).

For two opposing ideological perspectives on neoconservatism, see Irving Kristol, *Neoconservatism: The Autobiography of an Idea* (Ivan R. Dee, 1999); and John Ehrenberg, *Servants of Wealth: The Right's Attack on Economic Justice* (Rowman & Littlefield, 2006). For a representative anthology of neoconservative writings, see Irwin Stelzer (ed.), *The Neocon Reader* (Grove Press, 2004). Representative recent treatments of economic nationalism include Eric Helleiner and Andreas Pickel (eds.), *Economic Nationalism in* a *Globalizing World* (Cornell University Press, 2005); and Patrick J. Buchanan, *A Republic, Not an Empire: Reclaiming America's Destiny* (Regnery Press, 1999).

Chapter 3

We suggest the following further readings on Clinton's market globalism and Tony Blair's Third Way: David Stoesz, *Small Change: Domestic Policy under the Clinton Presidency* (Longman Publishers USA, 1996); Michael Meeropol, *Surrender: How the Clinton Administration Completed the Reagan Revolution* (University of Michigan Press, 1998); Daniel Yergin and Joseph Stanislaw, *The Commanding Heights: The Battle between Government and the Marketplace that is Remaking the Modern World* (Touchstone, 2002); and Bob Woodward, *The Agenda: Inside the Clinton White House* (Simon & Schuster Paperbacks, 2005); Anthony Giddens, *The Third Way: The Renewal of Social Democracy* (Polity Press, 1999) and *The Global Third Way Debate* (Polity, 2001); Flavio Romano, *Clinton and Blair: The Political Economy of the Third Way* (Routledge, 2006); Anthony Seldon, *Blair's Britain, 1997–2007* (Cambridge University Press, 2007); and Matt Beech and Simon Lee (eds.), *Ten Years of New Labour* (Palgrave Macmillan, 2008).

Our discussion of anti-trust policy in the Clinton era relies in part on Robert E. Litan and Carl Shapiro, 'Anti-Trust Policy in the Clinton Administration', in Jeffrey Frankel and Peter Orszag (eds.), *American Economic Policy in the 1990s* (Massachusetts Institute of Technology Press, 2002).

Readable books on globalization in the 1990s include: John Gray, *False Dawn: The Delusions of Global Capitalism* (The New Press, 1998); Edward Luttwak, *Turbo-Capitalism: Winners and Losers in the Global Economy* (HarperCollins Publishers, 1999); Thomas L. Friedman, *The Lexus and the Olive Tree* (Farrar, Straus, Giroux, 2000); Joseph E. Stiglitz, *The Roaring Nineties: A New History of the World's Most Prosperous Decade* (W. W. Norton, 2003) and *Globalization and its Discontents* (W. W. Norton, 2003).

For a general overview of globalization dynamics, see Manfred B. Steger, *Globalization: A Very Short Introduction*, 2nd edn. (Oxford University Press, 2009). The concept of 'soft power' has been pioneered by Joseph S. Nye, *Soft Power: The Means to Success in World Politics* (Public Affairs, 2004).

The text box in this chapter on neoliberal institutionalism was derived from Philip Cerny's discussion on the subject that appears in his article 'Embedding Neoliberalism: The Evolution of a Hegemonic Paradigm', *Journal of International Trade and Diplomacy* 2.1 (2008), pp. 1–46.

Our summary of the influence of neoliberal think tanks relies in part on Otto Singer, 'Knowledge and Politics in Economic Policy-Making: Official Economic Advisers in the USA, Britain and Germany', in B. Guy Peters and Anthony Barker (eds.), *Advising West European Governments: Inquiries, Expertise and Public Policy* (Edinburgh University Press, 1993).

Chapter 4

For an informative discussion of the Asian development model in the context of Japan, see Chalmers Johnson, *MITI and the Japanese Miracle: The Growth of Industrial Policy, 1925–1975* (Stanford University Press, 1982). The model's application to Taiwan, South Korea, and other newly industrializing countries is outlined in Robert Wade, *Governing the Market: Economic Theory and the Role of Government in East Asian Industrialization* (Princeton University Press, 1990).

Additional useful accounts of neoliberalization dynamics in Asia include: *The East Asian Miracle: Economic Growth and Public Policy*, A World Bank Policy Research Report (Oxford University Press, 1993); Jagdish Bhagwati, *India in Transition: Freeing the Economy* (Oxford University Press, 1993); Mayumi Itoh, *Globalization of Japan: Japanese Sakoku Mentality and US Efforts to Open Japan* (St Martin's Press, 1998); Aurelia George Mulgan, *Japan's Failed Revolution: Koizumi and the Politics of Economic Reform* (Asia Pacific Press, 2002); Fumio Iida, 'Kozo Kaikaku: The Emergence of Neoliberal Globalizations Discourse in Japan', in Manfred B. Steger, (ed.), *Rethinking Globalism* (Rowman & Littlefield, 2004); Arvind Panagariya, 'India in the 1980s and 1990s: A Triumph of Reforms', *IMF Working Paper*, WP/04/43, 2004; and Aihwa Ong, *Neoliberalism as Exception: Mutations in Citizenship and Sovereignty* (Duke University Press, 2006).

Our discussion of Chinese SOEs leans on David Harvey, *A Brief History of Neoliberalism* (Oxford University Press, 2005).

Our summary of neoliberal reforms enacted in India since 1991 relies on Sunil Rongala, 'Experiments with Neoliberalism in India: Shattering of Mental Model', in Ravi K. Roy, Arthur T. Denzau, and Thomas D. Willett (eds.), *Neoliberalism: National and Regional Experiments with Global Ideas* (Routledge, 2006).

Chapter 5

Our discussion in this chapter has greatly benefited from the arguments made by Naomi Klein, *The Shock Doctrine: The Rise of Disaster Capitalism* (Penguin Books, 2007). We also drew on useful ideas and arguments presented in: Anil Hira, *Ideas and Economic Policy in Latin America: Regional, National, and Organizational Case Studies* (Praeger, 1998) and *An East Asian Model for Latin American Success: The New Path* (Ashgate, 2007); J. L. Adedeji, 'The Legacy of J. J. Rawlings in Ghanaian Politics', *African Studies Quarterly* 5 (2001): online at: <http://web.africa.ufl.edu/asq/v5/v5i2a1.htm>; William K. Tabb, *The Amoral Elephant: Globalization and the Struggle for Social Justice in the Twenty-First Century* (Monthly Review Press, 2001); Ankie Hoogvelt, *Globalization and the Postcolonial World: A New Political Economy of Development*, 2nd edn. (The Johns Hopkins University Press, 2001); Dominick Salvatore, James W. Dean, and Thomas D. Willett (eds.), *The Dollarization Debate* (Oxford University Press, 2003); Sarah Babb, *Managing Mexico: Economists from Nationalism to Neoliberalism* (Princeton University Press, 2004); and James Ferguson, *Global Shadows: Africa in the Neoliberal World Order* (Duke University Press, 2006).

A radical, but riveting, account of the imposition of the Washington Consensus on the global South can be found in: John Perkins, *Confessions of an Economic Hit Man* (Penguin, 2005).

Chapter 6

For a description and analysis of the challengers of market globalism on the political Left and Right, see Manfred B. Steger, *Globalisms:*

The Great Ideological Struggle of the Twenty-First Century
(Rowman & Littlefield, 2009).

One of the best short accounts of the causes and consequences of the
global financial crisis has been authored by the Australian Prime
Minister Kevin Rudd. In his February 2009 article in *The Monthly*,
titled 'The Global Financial Crisis', he also engages in a severe
critique of neoliberalism. Moreover, the direct quotes from world
leaders in this chapter's relevant text box come from this article.
It can be accessed online at: <http://www.themonthly.com.au/tm/
print/1421>.

Some investment definitions were derived from *Black's Law
Dictionary*, 7th edn. (West Group, 1999).

The full text of the UNCTAD March 2009 Report, 'The Global
Economic Crisis: Systemic Failures and Multilateral Remedies', can
be accessed online at: <http://www.unctad.org/en/docs/
gds20091_en.pdf>.

The G-20 Communiqué of the 2009 London Summit can be accessed
online at: <http://www.londonsummit.gov.uk/resources/en/news/
15766232/communique-020409>.

The full text of the 2009 International Labour Organization Report can
be accessed at: <http://www.ilo.org/wcsmp5/groups/public/
dgreports/dcomm/documents/publication/wcms/_101461.pdf>.

The 2009 Zagat Report on Hotels, Resorts, and Spas can be accessed
online at: <http://www.zagat.com/About/Index.aspx?
menu=PR134>.

The full text of David Brooks' column, 'The Behavioral Revolution', can
be found at *New York Times* (28 October 2008).

Index

Afghanistan 47–8, 122–3
Africa 98, 110–18
airline deregulation 33–4
al-Qaeda 121–3
anti-globalization movement
    120–1, 123
Argentina 45–6, 99, 101–6
Asian development 57, 59, 76–97,
    105, 119, 133
Asian Financial Crisis 57, 77–8,
    105, 119, 133
Austrian School of Economics 15

bailout packages 127–9
Balkan Wars 72–4
'Big Bang' 42, 80–1
big government 1, 8–9, 17, 21, 40,
    48–9, 51
Big Mac index 89
Black Monday 32, 42
Blair, Tony 50, 51, 52, 66–75, 121
Bretton Woods 6
Brown, Gordon 67, 70, 133, 134
Bush, George HW 58–9, 70, 80
Bush, George W 55, 96, 121, 123

Calderón, Felipe 110
CEOs (chief executive officers),
    compensation packages of 60,
    61, 128

Chiapas uprising, Mexico 107–8,
    119
'Chicago Boys' 100, 102–3
Chicago School 17, 19, 99–103
Chile 19, 99–101, 107
China 10, 78–9, 83–90, 96, 135
class 7, 41, 67, 70–1, 100–1
classical liberalism 3, 5–6, 9, 11, 15
Clinton, Bill 50–66, 67, 69–70,
    72, 73, 75, 124
Cold War 27, 45
communism, fall of 10, 47, 53
comparative advantage, theory of 3
competition 62–3, 69, 79,
    87–8, 112
conservative values 14, 15, 22, 51
controlled capitalism, golden
    age of 7, 9
corporatism 77, 102
corruption 98, 108
credit crunch 129–30
credit ratings 124, 126
currency 68–9, 87–9, 98, 105, 108,
    114, 115 see also exchange
    rates

Dayton Agreement 73
debt 10, 19, 71, 105–7, 116, 117, 133
deficits 26–8, 34, 40, 58–9, 68,
    83, 96, 123

Democratic Leadership Council
(DLC) 64
Deng Xiaoping 84–6, 89–90
deregulation
Africa 110
Argentina 100, 102
D–L–P Formula 14, 136
global economic crisis 133
Thatcherism 42
Third Way 66–7
United States 31–4, 60, 124
Washington Consensus 20
developing countries
Africa 98, 110–18
Asian development 76–97
developmentalism 47, 99–100,
102, 105–6, 110
economic crises 131, 134
heavily indebted poor countries
(HIPCs) 10, 116, 117
International Monetary Fund 6
Latin America 19, 98, 99–110,
117–18
structural adjustment
programmes 10, 19, 53, 55, 94,
98, 103, 107, 110
developmentalism 47, 79–83,
99–100, 102, 105–6, 110
digital revolution 52–3
D–L–P Formula 14, 136

economic development 10, 19, 52
economic crises
Asian Financial Crisis 57, 77–8,
105, 119, 133
global economic crisis 1, 10, 33,
60, 106, 110, 118, 123–35
Ghana 115
Great Depression 1, 5, 9, 124, 135
India 93
Latin America 100, 102, 104–8
Marxism 5–6
Russia 57
economic nationalism 36, 80, 92,
93, 99

egalitarian liberalism 5, 9
elites 11, 53, 77, 82, 83, 98, 107–8,
119, 131
end of neoliberalism 1–2, 131–6
ethics in foreign policy 72–4
ethnic cleansing and genocide 73
European Union 40–1, 68–9,
73, 106
Eurozone 68–9
Exchange Rate Mechanism
(ERM) 40–1
exchange rates 29–30, 38, 40–1, 59,
69, 87–8, 92–3, 96, 103–4, 134

Falklands War 45–6, 102
financial institutions 81–3, 124–8,
133–5 see also International
Monetary Fund (IMF); World
Bank
financial instruments 31–2, 124–7,
133–5
financial services reform 42, 60,
80–1, 124
Financial Stability Board, proposal
for 134–5
first–wave neoliberalism
in 1980s 21–49, 51, 136–7
fiscal policy 17, 19, 26–30, 58–9,
64, 69–71, 94
foreign direct investment
(FDI) 68–9, 77–8, 85–7, 93,
96, 107, 111, 114–17
foreign policy 19, 27, 45–9, 55,
72–4, 121–2
free trade agreements 6–7, 10,
37–8, 46, 56, 107, 110, 136
Free Trade Area of the Americas
(FTAA), proposal for 38
Friedman, Milton 17, 18–19, 40,
83, 99, 100, 107, 110, 135

G–7 (Group of 7) 56–7
G–20 (Group of 20) 106, 134–5,
137
Gandhi, Indira 91–2

Gandhi, Rajiv 92–3
GATT (General Agreement on
    Tariffs and Trade) 6–7, 37, 56
Ghana 111–17
Giddens, Anthony 66–7
Glass–Steagall Act 124
global economic crisis 1, 10, 33, 60,
    106, 110, 118, 123–357
global jihadism 121–2
global justice movement
    120–1, 123
globalization 9, 11–12, 36, 49,
    52–4, 75, 80, 96, 110,
    119–23, 127
gold mining in Ghana 114–15
Gorbachev, Mikhail 46–8
governance 11, 12–14, 30, 34–5
government spending 6, 9–10,
    27–8, 38–9, 58, 67–70
Gramm–Rudman–Hollings
    Initiative (GRH) 28
Great Depression 1, 5, 9, 124, 135
Greenspan, Alan 29, 58–9, 70,
    124, 131

hard power and soft power 54–5
Hashimoto, Ryutaro 78–9, 80–1
Hayek, Friedrich von 15–17, 83,
    100, 135
healthcare 35, 44–5, 66, 71
heavily indebted poor countries
    (HIPCs) 10, 116, 117
housing 29, 33, 41, 96, 125
Hu Jintao 78–9, 90
human rights 72–3, 75
humanitarianism 72–4

Icelandic meltdown 128–9
ideology 10–15, 20–2, 30, 46–8, 53,
    67, 84, 119, 131, 135
income 7, 60, 61–3, 65–6, 70–2, 128
India 78–9, 90–6, 135
inequality and poverty 41, 53, 57,
    75, 90–1, 100–1, 108, 114,
    117, 120

inflation
    Asian financial crisis 78
    debt 133
    Ghana 114, 117
    interest rates 14, 29, 40, 58
    Keynesian 9, 10, 17
    Latin America 100–6
    Maastricht Treaty 69
    monetarism 17, 27, 29
innovative instruments 124 7
Intel 63
intellectual origins of
    neoliberalism 15–20
interest rates 14, 29, 40, 58–9, 70,
    78, 81, 98, 114
International Monetary Fund
    (IMF) 73, 119–20, 134–6
    Bretton Woods 6
    Ghana 110, 112
    India 93–4
    Latin America 103–5, 107
    loans 10, 19, 98
    structural adjustment
        programmes 53, 98, 107, 110
    Washington Consensus 19–20,
        56–7, 117–18
Iraq 122–3

Japan 35, 78–83, 130
Jiang Zemin 78–9, 90

Keynes, John Maynard 5–10, 15,
    17, 19–21, 38, 43–4, 48–50, 60,
    71, 99, 135, 137
Kirchner, Nestor and Cristina 38,
    105–6
Koizumi, Junichiro 78–9, 81–3
Kosovo 73–4
Kufuor, John 117

labour force 34, 43, 77, 80, 86–7,
    93, 115, 120, 135
Laffer Curve 24
Latin America 19, 59, 98, 99–110,
    117–18

liberalization 14, 19–20, 37–8, 51,
    53–4, 56–7, 91, 92, 110, 114,
    119, 136
libertarianism 17
List, Friedrich 36
loans 10, 19, 57, 81, 92–3, 98, 102,
    114, 125
Locke, John 5
London bombings 7 July, 2005
    122

macroeconomics 9, 69, 99
Mao Zedong 83–4
market globalism 51–66, 67–9, 75,
    82, 90–6, 111, 121, 123
Marxism 5, 12, 15, 91
mass production 7
media 11–12, 23, 52–3
Menem, Carlos 46, 102–4, 112
Mexico 99, 104, 106, 110
Microsoft 63
military spending 27–9, 45,
    47–9, 51
monetarism 17, 23, 25, 27,
    38–40, 81
monetary policy 29, 38–40, 59, 70,
    94, 103–4, 125
monopolies 62–3
Mont Pelerin Society 15, 17
mortgages 29, 33, 125–7

NAFTA (North American Free
    Trade Agreement) 37–8, 56,
    107, 110
National Health Service
    (NHS) 44–5, 71
nationalism 36, 45, 80, 92, 93,
    99
nationalization 92, 99, 105–6, 127
NATO 72–4
Nehru, Jawaharlal 91–2, 93, 96
neoconservatism 14, 22–3, 45–6,
    51, 55, 121–2
New Deal 7, 60, 71
New Democrats 64–5, 67

New Economy 64, 66–7
New Federalism 30–2
New Labour 50, 67–71
new public management
    (NPM) 13–14, 30, 44
Nkrumah, Kwame 111–12
nuclear power in India 95–6
Nye Jr, Joseph 55

Obama, Barack 1–2, 134

patriotism 45, 51
pensions 31, 43–4
Perónists 102–3, 105
Pinochet, Augusto 100–1, 107
price controls 17, 99, 100, 105
privatization
    Africa 98
    Asian development 76
    China 86
    D–L–P Formula 14, 136
    Ghana 110, 114–15
    India 94, 96
    Japan 81–3
    Latin America 98, 100, 103
    Thatcher administration 38,
        41, 75
    United States 34, 57, 75
protectionism 3, 35–6, 77, 79, 106,
    111–12, 121
public choice theory 30
public policies 11, 14–15, 21, 30
public–private sector
    cooperation 77, 79, 94–5, 134

Rao, Narashima 93
Rawlings, Jerry 112–14
Reaganomics 20, 21–38, 40, 44–9,
    51, 57, 59, 60, 64, 65, 70, 75,
    123–4
real estate 32–4, 123, 133
regulatory reform 14, 76, 124,
    133–6 *see also* deregulation
rescue packages 127–9
Ricardo, David 2, 3

Roosevelt, Franklin D 6, 7, 60, 124
Russia 56–7, 105, 119

Salinas de Gatari, Carlos 107–8
Sarkozy, Nicolas 133, 134
Savings & Loans (S&L) 31, 32–3,
    57–8
second–wave neoliberalism in
    1990s 50–75, 121, 137
securities 124–7
security 72–3, 121–2
self–regulating market 2, 11, 12, 15,
    17, 20, 54, 131
September 11, 2001 terrorist
    attacks on United States
    121–3
Singh, Manmohan 78–9, 91, 93–6
Smith, Adam 2–3, 4
social class 7, 41, 67, 70–1, 100–1
social justice 12, 56, 59, 64, 68, 75
social policy 34–5, 50, 64, 75
social security 7, 9, 35, 43–4, 64–5,
    71–2, 99
Soviet Union 10, 45–8, 53, 56, 91
Special Enterprise Zones (SEZs)
    (China) 87–8
stagflation 9, 26, 119
Stiglitz, Joseph 55
stimulus packages 134–5
structural adjustment programmes
    (SAPs) 10, 19, 53, 55, 94, 98,
    103, 107, 110
subprime mortgages 33, 125–7
super or turbo capitalism 51, 62, 75
supply-side economics 23–5, 27

takeovers and mergers 31–2, 60
Tata Motors 91
tax 17, 19, 24–9, 38–9, 57, 59–60,
    64, 69–71, 92, 94, 105,
    114–15
telecommunications 60, 62
terrorism 96, 121–3
Thatcherism 20, 21–3, 25, 27, 34,
    38–51, 67, 70–1, 137

Third Way 50, 52, 66–72, 75
three dimensions of
    neoliberalism 11–14
Tiananmen Square massacre
    88–9
trade organizations and
    agreements 6–7, 10, 37–8
trade unions 7, 34, 38, 42, 103, 112
transnational corporations
    (TNCs) 52–3, 91, 98, 114
Tsingtao Brewery 87

UNCTAD Report 'Global Economic
    Crisis' 131, 133–4
unemployment 6, 9, 26, 42, 64, 71,
    114, 130–1
United Kingdom 3–4, 6
    first-wave neoliberalism 21–4,
        38–49, 136–7
    foreign policy 45–9, 72–4, 121–2
    second–wave neoliberalism
        50–1, 66–75, 137
    Third Way 52, 66–72
United States 1–2, 6–8, 14, 17
    first-wave neoliberalism 21–38,
        45–9, 136
    foreign policy 19, 27, 45–9, 55,
        72–4, 121–2
    global economic crisis 123–33
    India Civil Nuclear Deal 96
    Latin America 19, 59, 99–100,
        103, 110
    market globalism 51–66
    second–wave
        neoliberalism 50–66, 72–5, 137
    terrorism 121–3
Uruguay Round 37, 56

Volcker, Paul 29

Washington Consensus 19–20,
    56, 90, 98–9, 106–7, 110,
    117–19, 136
welfare 7, 9, 35, 43–4, 64–5, 71–2,
    99

Index

World Bank 73, 118–19, 131, 135–6
  Asian development 76
  Bretton Woods 6
  Latin America 98, 117
  structural adjustment policies 53, 55, 98, 110–11, 115
  Washington Consensus 19–20

World Trade Organization (WTO) 6–7, 10, 37, 56, 73, 90, 120, 136

Yeltsin, Boris 56–7

Zapatistas 107–8, 119
Zedillo Ponce de León, Ernesto 107–10

Neoliberalism